AS/A-LEVEL YEAR 1

STUDENT GUIDE

OCR

Economics

Microeconomics 1

Sam Dobin

PHILIP ALLAN FOR
HODDER
EDUCATION
AN HACHETTE UK COMPANY

Philip Allan, an imprint of Hodder Education, an Hachette UK company, Blenheim Court, George Street, Banbury, Oxfordshire OX16 5BH

Orders

Bookpoint Ltd, 130 Milton Park, Abingdon, Oxfordshire OX14 4SB

tel: 01235 827827

fax: 01235 400401

e-mail: education@bookpoint.co.uk

Lines are open 9.00 a.m.–5.00 p.m., Monday to Saturday, with a 24-hour message answering service. You can also order through the Hodder Education website: www.hoddereducation. co.uk

© Sam Dobin 2015

ISBN 978-1-4718-4417-1

First printed 2015

Impression number 5 4 3 2 1

Year 2019 2018 2017 2016 2015

This Guide has been written specifically to support students preparing for the OCR AS and A-level Economics examinations. The content has been neither approved nor endorsed by OCR and remains the sole responsibility of the author.

Typeset by Integra Software Services Pvt. Ltd., Pondicherry, India

Cover photo: Iakov Kalinin/Fotolia

Printed in Italy

Hachette UK's policy is to use papers that are natural, renewable and recyclable products and made from wood grown in sustainable forests. The logging and manufacturing processes are expected to conform to the environmental regulations of the country of origin.

Contents

■ Getting the most from this book

Exam-style questions

Commentary on the questions

Tips on what you need to do to gain full marks, indicated by the icon ⓔ

Sample student answers

Practise the questions, then look at the student answers that follow.

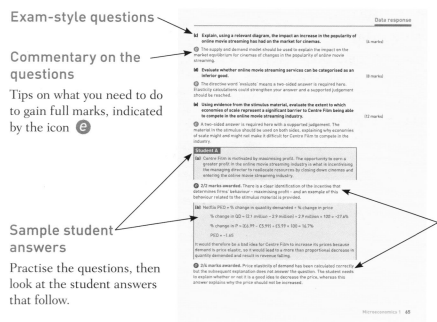

Commentary on sample student answers

Find out how many marks each answer would be awarded in the exam and then read the comments (preceded by the icon ⓔ) following each student answer. Annotations that link back to points made in the student answers show exactly how and where marks are gained or lost.

■About this book

This guide is designed to prepare you for the AS and A-level OCR microeconomics exams. The guide covers all of the content required to sit the AS exam and approximately half of the content required to sit the A-level exam. It includes sample questions and answers to prepare you for both papers.

The guide is split into two sections:

Content Guidance

This section explains the core microeconomics concepts required to excel in this course. This can be split into three broad topic areas:

- Scarcity and choice
- How competitive markets work
- Market failure and government intervention

You should make sure you have fully mastered all of the content in this guide before progressing onto the practice questions. Use the knowledge checks as you work through the guide to test your understanding and take on board the exam tips to avoid falling into the traps that most commonly result in students losing marks. At the end of each topic area there is a bullet-pointed summary of the content covered – if you are unable to offer a detailed explanation of any part of this, you should read the section again to clear up any misunderstanding.

Questions & Answers

This section begins by setting out the format of the AS and A-level OCR microeconomics exam papers. It gives you advice on how long to spend on each question and offers important tips on how to maximise your marks on the different elements of the paper. It also explains the levels system used to mark essays.

This is followed by a series of sample questions, covering all the different types of assessment seen in both the AS and A-level papers – multiple-choice, data response and essays. After all these questions there are some example answers from students. You should practise all these questions yourself and compare your answers to the example answers while reading the detailed exam advice to improve your understanding of what is required to achieve full marks.

Content Guidance

■ Scarcity and choice

The basic economic problem

The basic economic problem exists because resources are scarce and wants are infinite. Economists are therefore tasked with making choices which efficiently allocate these scarce resources. The key insight from the basic economic problem is that we cannot have everything that we want — this is true on a household, firm and governmental level:

- Households have a scarce amount of income and have to make choices as to how to allocate this income, e.g. whether to buy a new car or go on holiday.
- Firms in the short run have a limited amount of resources and have to make choices as to how to allocate these resources, e.g. a clothes manufacturer has to decide whether to use its labour to produce t-shirts or jeans.
- Governments have insufficient tax revenue to meet the public service demands of the whole population and therefore have to make spending decisions, e.g. whether to build a new hospital or increase teachers' wages.

Allocation decisions are required for all economic goods. These represent the vast majority of goods in society. The exception is free goods, for which no allocation decision is required because there is no scarcity of the good.

All goods and services in the economy are produced by a combination of the four factors of production:

- Labour is the human input into the production process.
- Capital is any man-made aid to production.
- Enterprise is the risk taking involved in organising the other factors of production.
- Land is a natural resource – it includes the physical land itself and everything that occurs naturally on it.

Positive and normative statements

As economists, we need to be able to differentiate between positive and normative economic statements.

- Positive statements are objective statements that can be tested using evidence.
- Normative statements are subjective statements based on value judgements that cannot be proven.

Words such as 'should', 'right', 'wrong', 'best' and 'worst' often imply a value judgement is being made and therefore can help identify normative statements.

Exam tip

Do not confuse needs with wants in your definition of the basic economic problem. Needs are not infinite and in the developed world there are often sufficient resources to meet the population's needs.

Knowledge check 1

What are the rewards of each of the factors of production?

Opportunity cost

The economic problem results in there being an **opportunity cost** to most decisions taken – making a choice usually involves an element of sacrifice. A production possibility frontier (PPF) diagram can be used to illustrate the concept of opportunity cost (see Figure 1).

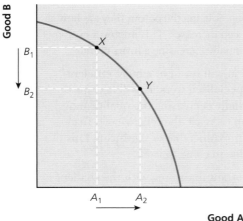

Figure 1 Production possibility frontier

Suppose the economy is initially at point X, producing B_1 units of good B and B_2 units of good A. To increase the production of good A, production can move along the PPF from X to Y. The result is that the production of A has increased from A_1 to A_2. However, to achieve this, the production of some of B has to be sacrificed $(B_2 - B_1)$.

Thus, the opportunity cost of producing $(A_2 - A_1)$ units of good A is the sacrifice of $(B_2 - B_1)$ units of good B. Because all resources are fully and efficiently employed when on the PPF, the only way to increase the output of one good is to reallocate resources and in doing so sacrifice some output of the other good.

In the long run, it is possible for the PPF to shift outwards as a result of an increase in the quality or quantity of factors of production. For example, technological advancement could increase the quality of capital, boosting the productive capacity of the economy and causing the PPF to shift to the right.

Specialisation and trade

Specialisation can take place on an individual, a firm and a national level. It can be seen as an important tool in addressing the problem of scarcity – specialisation is a route through which more output can be produced with a given set of inputs, which can increase the number of wants and needs that can be satisfied.

One form of specialisation is the division of labour. This takes place within a firm, where individual workers are responsible for performing specialised tasks. There are clear advantages to this – it is likely the tasks they are specialised in are those they are best at conducting (for example, an individual specialising as an economics teacher is likely to be more skilled teaching economics than drama because they have relevant

Opportunity cost
The sacrifice of the next best alternative foregone when a choice is made.

Exam tip

Be careful not to make the mistake of saying that point X or point Y is more efficient – remember, all points on the PPF are productively efficient. This means productive efficiency would still be achieved even if the economy was operating at either end of the PPF (i.e. when the output of either good A or good B was zero).

Knowledge check 2

Explain whether there is an opportunity cost to increasing output when an economy is operating inside its PPF.

skills and qualifications related to economics) and that, over time, these skills will increase through the process of repetition. This benefits the firm for two reasons:

- *Increased output* – because specialised workers are able to produce output at a quicker rate (as a result of the increased skill that comes from repeating the same task), firms' output is likely to increase. This will enable firms to generate greater revenue and profit than before specialisation took place.
- *Improved quality* – when workers are specialised in producing the output they are best at producing, the quality of the good or service produced increases. This improves customer satisfaction, increasing demand and therefore potentially increasing a firm's profit.

However, it is not always the case that specialisation will result in a more efficient use of scarce resources. There is a risk that over-specialised workers will become bored, reducing productivity and as a result potentially decreasing the quality and quantity of output. Furthermore, specialisation can increase the reliance of a firm on one particular worker, which could leave the firm vulnerable to significant falls in productivity if for any reason that worker was unable to come to work.

While specialisation can therefore be seen as important in dealing with the challenges posed by scarcity, it has its limitations and needs to be practised with caution.

Exam tip

When asked to explain the benefits of specialisation to a firm, ensure you always clearly identify why these benefits result from specialisation. It is not enough to say quality increases because workers are 'specialised' – you must explain the impact of this.

Gains from trade

The theory of specialisation provides a powerful argument in favour of trade taking place within and between economies. The famous 'Robinson Crusoe' example can be used to illustrate this. Suppose two individuals (A and B) are living on an island. Assuming they have a sufficient supply of water and shelter, they require two goods to survive – food and fuel. If each individual produces both goods, they will be able to produce 100 units of food and 100 units of fuel. However, if individuals A and B were to specialise in producing the good they are most efficient at producing, individual A would be able to produce 300 units of food and individual B would be able to produce 300 units of fuel. Through specialisation, then, total output of each good has increased by 50%.

In order for the individuals to benefit from this increase in total output, they will need to engage in trade. If through bartering they agree to exchange one unit of food for one unit of fuel, they will each be able to enjoy the consumption of 150 units of food and 150 units of fuel.

The same logic can be used to explain the concept of international trade. By countries specialising in the production of the goods and services they are most efficient at producing, world output increases and through trade, consumers in these countries are able to enjoy a higher standard of living than they would be able to without specialisation. On a global level, then, specialisation can also enable the world's scarce resources to be used more efficiently.

Knowledge check 3

Can you think of any disadvantages of international specialisation?

The role of money

The problem with trade taking place through bartering is that there is a double coincidence of wants – the person who has what you want has to be willing to exchange it for what you have. In practice, this makes trade extremely difficult to conduct.

Money therefore serves to facilitate trade. It acts as a medium of exchange – even if the person who has the good or service you want does not want the good or service you are producing, you are still able to trade with them by exchanging the good or service you desire for money. The person you are buying from is willing to accept this as a form of payment because they know this money will be accepted by another producer in exchange for the good or service they want.

There are several other advantages of using money within an economy:

- *Store of value* – as long as there is not hyperinflation, money provides a method for saving wealth for the future. This would not be possible without money if all of your wealth was held in perishable assets – for example, a farmer would not be able to store eggs to retain wealth for the future as those eggs would become worthless over time.
- *Unit of account* – money allows the value of different goods and services to be compared in a way that everyone can understand easily.
- *Standard of deferred payment* – individuals and firms can make agreements for the future, which are often expressed in money terms. For example, workers agree to supply their labour knowing they will receive a deferred payment (their wage) at the end of the month.

Summary

After studying the topic of *Scarcity and choice* you should be able to:

- Understand that the basic economic problem results from the problem of scarcity.
- Explain the difference between needs and wants.
- Recognise the difference between a positive and a normative economic statement.
- Identify the four factors of production and give applied examples of them in different markets.

- Understand the concept of opportunity cost and be able to illustrate it on a PPF diagram.
- Explain what is meant by specialisation and the division of labour.
- Evaluate the role of specialisation in addressing the problem of scarcity.
- Understand how specialisation encourages trade and exchange in an economy.
- Understand how money facilitates trade and exchange.

How competitive markets work

Allocation of resources

The role of incentives

The basic economic problem illustrates to us that it is not possible to meet all of the wants that exist within an economy due to the scarcity of resources. Because there are a limited number of factors of production, decisions have to be taken over how these resources are allocated to determine which goods and services will be produced and therefore which wants will be met.

The process of allocating resources therefore has to answer three fundamental questions:

- What to produce?
- How to produce?
- For whom to produce?

In most economies, households, firms and governments are all involved in decisions regarding the allocation of resources. Each of these economic agents is motivated by different concerns – these factors that determine decision making are known as incentives.

One of the most powerful incentives is the price of a product. When deciding whether to spend scarce income on a good or service, households will consider whether consuming it will derive sufficient benefit compared with the price to justify its purchase. Households will also use the price of the product to determine the opportunity cost of consumption – they will consume the good only if they derive more benefit than they would do from consuming a good that is similarly priced but that has to be sacrificed in order to consume the good.

Firms are also incentivised by the price. When households are willing to pay a high price for a good, this sends a signal to firms that they should be allocating more of their resources towards the production of that product. Given the power the price of a product can have on consumption and production decisions, the government often pursues measures designed to impact on the price of goods or services in an attempt to influence incentives.

However, price is not the only incentive that impacts on the behaviour of economic agents. For example, households are more likely to consume goods and services to which they have easy access (meaning location and availability impact on their incentives). Firms will also consider the cost of producing goods and services when deciding where to allocate their scarce resources (a good that demands a high price but is very costly to produce will not necessarily provide strong incentives to a firm).

Economic systems

The relative power of different economic agents in the resource allocation process is largely determined by the economic system a country operates.

- *Market economy* – resources are owned and allocated by private individuals and firms. The price mechanism is crucial to the allocation of resources – an increase in the price consumers are willing to pay will signal to firms to allocate more scarce resources to the production of the product, while a decrease in the price will signal to firms to allocate fewer resources to the production of the product. The government has little role to play in a market economy, with decisions taken by millions of agents motivated by their own satisfaction. This system of resource allocation is known as **capitalism**.
- *Centrally planned economy* – resources are owned and allocated by the government. In such economic systems production boards meet to decide the level of output for a whole industry and then set targets for firms which they must meet.

The most famous example of a centrally planned economy was the Soviet Union in the twentieth century. Communists argued that the market economy was an inappropriate way to allocate resources because it was driven by self-interest, which neglected the needs of the whole of society. This led to much of the population suffering because they did not have the power to influence decision making, meaning their interests were subsequently ignored.

Knowledge check 4

How would the incentives of households and firms be affected by a fall in the price of a product?

Capitalism A system of production in which there is private ownership of productive resources, and individuals are free to pursue their objectives with minimal interference from government.

While such self-interest can produce some valid criticisms of the market economy, central planning is largely accepted to be an inefficient solution. Without the price mechanism to send signals, centrally planned economies are often characterised by shortages and surpluses in the production of many goods and services, with production rarely matching consumer demand. Few countries continue to operate with a centrally planned economy – North Korea and Cuba are notable exceptions.

Given the potential drawbacks of both market and centrally planned economic systems, most countries operate a mixed economy. The advantage of this system is that it enables most resource allocation to benefit from the efficiency the market mechanism brings while enabling the government to protect the welfare of society by allocating resources that are considered basic rights or needs, such as education and healthcare. The balance between public and private provision varies significantly between countries, but there is a general trend towards privatisation, with resources being transferred from government to private ownership.

The objectives of economic agents

The decisions economic agents make are largely determined by their objectives. These can be summarised as follows:

- *Households* – decide which goods and services to consume based on the *satisfaction* the consumption will bring them.
- *Firms* – decide to produce goods and services based on the *profit* they will earn from production.
- *Governments* – make decisions based on what will deliver the best outcome for society; they are concerned about *social welfare*.

Furthermore, we assume that these economic agents behave according to the principles of maximisation. If this were the case, households would make decisions that result in them enjoying the most satisfaction possible – for example, their decision as to whether to go out to a restaurant or the cinema would be determined by which option they would enjoy the most. Maximisation would also suggest firms aim to maximise profit and that governments would make decisions that would deliver the best outcome in terms of social welfare.

However, while maximisation may seem rational, there is strong evidence that economic agents do not always adopt such a strategy when making decisions. This is partly because, in reality, their objectives are much more complex than those previously suggested. For example, you may be choosing to revise for an Economics exam rather than play a computer game, even though you may derive more satisfaction from playing the computer game. This may be because you are choosing to sacrifice satisfaction now for the long-term satisfaction of better career prospects from performing well in school.

The extent to which households are motivated by future benefits, then, can determine decisions made in the present. Moreover, households also make decisions about how to allocate their time. Many individuals may choose employment that is less satisfying than alternative employment because of the higher wage it commands.

It is equally difficult to interpret government behaviour as maximising social welfare. This is because governments have a range of complex concerns to consider when making decisions. While providing free gym membership to the whole population

Knowledge check 5

Summarise the costs and benefits of privatisation.

might improve social welfare, this comes at the cost of cutting spending in other areas or increasing tax rates. Different governments interpret how to go about maximising social welfare very differently. For example, while most developed countries provide free primary and secondary education, few countries choose to provide healthcare for free in the way the NHS does in Britain.

Knowledge check 6

Why might firms not engage in profit-maximising behaviour?

Supply and demand and the interaction of markets

Demand

The concept of demand illustrates the quantity of a good or service consumers will purchase at different prices. In economics, we are interested in studying market demand. This is simply found by adding together the demand from all individuals at any particular price. For example, suppose you would not consume any chocolate at a price of £1 a bar, but there are 200,000 people who would consume an average of two bars each at that price. At a price of £1, your individual demand would be zero and the market demand would be 400,000.

You need to understand the following different types of demand:

- *Derived demand* – demand is determined by the output it produces. For example, demand for labour will increase when the demand for the output it produces increases.
- *Joint demand* – demand is determined by the demand for another good or service. For example, the demand for computer games is positively correlated to the demand for computers.
- *Composite demand* – demand has multiple uses. For example, mobile phones are demanded for multiple uses, such as to make calls, browse the internet and play games.
- *Competitive demand* – demand is in competition with demand for another good or service. For example, demand for laptops is in competition with demand for tablets.

It is crucial to understand the difference between a movement along the demand curve and a shift of the demand curve (see Figure 2).

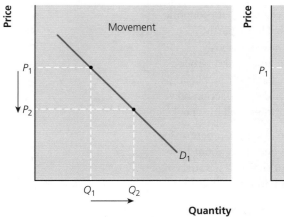
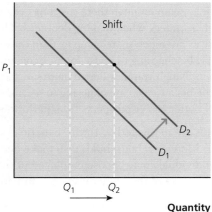

Figure 2 Movement along the demand curve

Movements along the demand curve show how quantity demanded responds to a change in price. The law of demand tells us there is an inverse relationship between price and quantity demanded. As illustrated in the left-hand figure, a decrease in the price from P_1 to P_2 will cause an increase in quantity demanded from Q_1 to Q_2. This illustrates an extension along the demand curve and occurs because a fall in the price will cause existing consumers to purchase more of the good and/or new consumers to enter the market.

Exam tip

The word 'quantity' is crucial when explaining movements along the demand curve. 'Demand' represents the whole demand schedule (i.e. the different levels of quantity demanded at different prices). Demand therefore does not change when the price changes – there is the same level of quantity demanded at any given price, but the price has changed, causing a change in quantity demanded.

Shifts of the demand curve show how demand responds to a change in a non-price factor. The figure on the right illustrates how the quantity demanded has increased at any given price as a result of the demand curve shifting to the right. In other words, the price has remained constant (at P_1) but the quantity demanded has increased (from Q_1 to Q_2), demonstrating this increase in demand must have resulted from a factor other than price.

There are four non-price factors you need to know which explain why the demand curve may shift to the right:

■ *Increase in income* – individuals can afford to purchase more normal and luxury goods, meaning the demand for such goods increases.
■ *Increase in the price of substitutes* – makes the product relatively cheaper, causing consumers to switch away from the substitute and demand more of the product.
■ *Decrease in the price of complements* – because complements are jointly demanded, this decreases the overall price of consuming the goods, causing the demand for the product to increase.
■ *Changes in tastes and fashion* – an increase in popularity will make the product more desirable, causing demand to increase.

A decrease in income, fall in the price of substitutes, increase in the price of substitutes and change in tastes and fashion would all explain why demand for a product may decrease.

Consumer surplus

The demand curve illustrates how different individuals are willing to pay different amounts to consume particular products – those who value the product highly will be willing to pay a higher price than someone who derives less satisfaction from consuming the product. Because firms are unable to charge different prices to different consumers (largely because there is no way of identifying the price any one consumer is willing to pay for the product due to asymmetric information), all individuals who are willing to pay more than the market price for a product enjoy some **consumer surplus**.

Knowledge check 7

Draw a contraction along the demand curve and a decrease in demand.

Exam tip

Ensure you always apply your analysis of the non-price factor to the market in the question. To do this you should give an example of a substitute or complementary good, or give a relevant explanation as to why the particular product in the question might become more popular.

Consumer surplus The difference between the price consumers are willing to pay for a product and the market price.

Diagrammatically, this can be illustrated by shading in the triangle representing the area under the demand curve and above the price line. In the exam, you will need to be able to analyse the impact on consumer surplus of an increase or a decrease in the price. An increase in the price will reduce the gap between the price consumers are willing to pay and the market price, thus decreasing consumer surplus. This can be illustrated in Figure 3, where consumer surplus decreases by area ABP_1P_2.

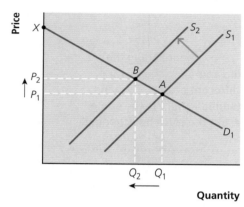

Figure 3 A decrease in consumer surplus

When evaluating the impact of an increase in price on consumer surplus, it is important to consider the size of the increase in price – the larger the increase in price, the greater the reduction in consumer surplus. The price elasticity of demand is another relevant factor. When demand is price elastic there is unlikely to be much consumer surplus enjoyed initially; any increase in price is likely to eliminate the majority of it, as many consumers will stop purchasing the good. When demand is price inelastic, the initial level of consumer surplus will be high; an increase in price will therefore result in a significant decrease in consumer surplus but is still likely to leave a significant amount of consumer surplus in the market, providing the increase in price is not too substantial.

Supply

Goods and services are produced by firms, which decide how much to supply based on the level of profit they can earn from producing the product. This therefore explains the positive relationship between quantity supplied and the price – the higher the price, the greater the profit a firm can make from supplying the good and thus the more it is willing to supply. Adding the quantity supplied of all individual firms at each price generates a market supply curve.

You need to understand the following different types of supply:

- *Joint supply* – firms produce the product alongside another product. For example, firms that supply computer processors are also likely to supply monitors.
- *Composite supply* – firms produce a product that has multiple sources of demand. For example, a firm supplying rubber receives demand from both car and shoe manufacturers.
- *Competitive supply* – firms can choose to reallocate their factors of production used to supply one good to supply another.

> **Exam tip**
>
> Draw a diagram when evaluating changes in consumer surplus in the exam. By shifting the supply curve to the left you can illustrate the different changes in consumer surplus when the price increases by drawing two separate diagrams, one with an elastic demand curve and the other with an inelastic demand curve.

It is crucial to understand the difference between a movement along the supply curve and a shift of the supply curve (see Figure 4).

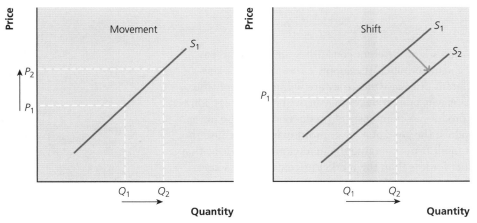

Figure 4 A movement and a shift along the supply curve

Movements along the supply curve show how quantity supplied responds to a change in price. As illustrated in the left-hand figure, an increase in the price from P_1 to P_2 will cause an increase in quantity supplied from Q_1 to Q_2. This shows an extension along the supply curve and occurs because an increase in the price will cause existing producers to supply more of the product and/or new firms to enter the market because of the increased profitability of supplying the good.

Shifts of the supply curve show how supply responds to a change in a non-price factor. The figure on the right illustrates how the quantity supplied has increased at any given price as a result of the supply curve shifting to the right. In other words, the price has remained constant (at P_1) but the quantity supplied has increased (from Q_1 to Q_2), demonstrating this increase in supply must have resulted from a factor other than price.

There are several non-price factors you need to know which explain why the supply curve may shift to the right:

- *Decrease in the costs of production* – when the product becomes less expensive to make, its profitability increases, meaning firms are more willing and able to supply the product.
- *Improvement in technology* – technological developments can help improve the efficiency of production, lowering the costs of production and causing the impact on supply described above.
- *Decrease in indirect taxes and increase in subsidy* – action by the government can affect supply of a product. When the government decreases the tax charged on a product it means firms have to give less of their revenue to the government. When a subsidy is granted or increased it increases the revenue firms receive from the government, which can help reduce costs of production.
- *A decrease in the price of goods in competitive supply* – a decrease in the price of another good which is in competitive supply could cause supply of a product to increase, as firms find it more profitable to reallocate their factors of production to producing the product.
- *Expectations of future price rises* – as supply cannot adjust instantaneously, expectations of high returns from supplying the product in the future can cause the supply of the product to increase immediately.

Knowledge check 8

What impact would an increase in the price of plastic have on the supply of mobile phones?

Exam tip

Most shifts in supply in the exam can be related back to costs of production. This is the most significant non-price factor affecting supply, as firms' profits are ultimately determined by revenue (which is dictated by demand) and costs.

An increase in the costs of production, increase in indirect tax, decrease in subsidy, increase in the price of goods in competitive supply and expectation of future price cuts would all explain why the supply of a product might decrease.

Producer surplus

Just as the demand curve illustrates how different consumers are willing to pay different prices to consume the same product, the supply curve illustrates how different producers have a different price at which they are willing to supply the product. There are many reasons why one producer may be willing to accept a lower price for a good than another producer – their costs of production might be lower or they might be willing to produce the good at a lower profit margin. Because the market mechanism will result in all firms charging the market price, all firms that are willing to supply the product for less than the market price will enjoy some **producer surplus**.

Diagrammatically, it can be illustrated by shading in the triangle representing the area above the supply curve and below the price line. In the exam, you will need to be able to analyse the impact of an increase or a decrease in the price on producer surplus. An increase in the price will increase the gap between the market price and the price producers are willing to receive for the product, thus increasing producer surplus. This can be illustrated in Figure 5, where producer surplus increases by area ABP_2P_1.

Producer surplus The difference between the market price and the price at which producers are willing to supply their product.

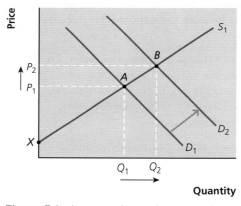

Figure 5 An increase in producer surplus

As with consumer surplus, both the size of the change in price and elasticity will determine the impact changes in price have on producer surplus. The increase in producer surplus will be greatest when supply is inelastic, as producers who were already in the market and were willing to supply the good for a far lower price now see further increases in producer surplus.

Knowledge check 9

Will producer surplus ever be negative?

Market equilibrium

Equilibrium in product markets

In a market, the price mechanism exists to ensure that markets clear, with an equilibrium reached where quantity supplied equals quantity demanded. The situations of disequilibrium illustrated in Figure 6 can be used to explain how the market adjusts to reach an equilibrium.

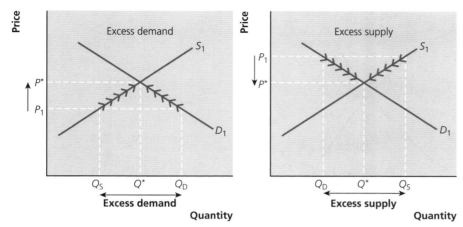

Figure 6 Disequilibrium in a market

Suppose we are considering a local bakery. When the price of bread is below the market clearing price, there is a situation of excess demand. This is because there is a greater quantity demanded of bread (Q_D) than the number of loaves of bread supplied (Q_S) at the low price. In practice, this means that each day the baker will run out of bread before the end of the day. Observing this high level of demand, the baker will respond by increasing the price of bread. This will cause a contraction along the demand curve – fewer consumers will be willing to purchase the bread at a higher price – and an extension along the supply curve, as the baker will be prepared to supply more bread at a higher price. The price will continue to increase until a price of P^* is reached, where quantity supplied equals quantity demanded and the market clears.

The same logic can be used to explain how the market mechanism works to eliminate excess supply. When the price of bread is above the market clearing price and there is excess supply, the baker will decrease the price of bread in an attempt to sell some of the leftover supply. This will cause a contraction along the supply curve and an extension along the demand curve until a price of P^* is reached.

However, it should be noted that disequilibriums can persist in the long run in some markets. This most often occurs when the government intervenes in markets, perhaps by setting a maximum or minimum price. While this will result in allocative inefficiency, disequilibrium is not necessarily an undesirable outcome. An example of this is the disequilibrium that existed in the market for tickets during the London 2012 Olympic Games. While some would argue fixing prices below the market equilibrium generated inefficiency, others would suggest that this was a worthwhile price to pay for the resulting increased fairness that gave millions more people the chance to bid for tickets to watch events.

Equilibrium in other markets

The model of supply and demand can also be used to explain how equilibrium is reached in other markets. In labour markets, equilibrium is determined by the supply of and demand for labour. As illustrated in Figure 7, if the wage rate was too high at W_1, a situation of excess supply would result in the wage rate falling. In this situation, individuals without jobs would be willing to work for lower than the going wage rate, meaning employers would reduce the wage rate until equilibrium was achieved at a wage rate of W^*.

Knowledge check 10

Why would the government want to intervene in a market to set the price above the market equilibrium to create a situation of excess supply?

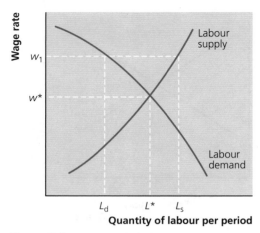

Figure 7 Excess supply in the labour market

Figure 8 illustrates that equilibrium in money markets is also determined by the forces of supply and demand. We assume here that the money supply curve is vertical as it is controlled by the Bank of England and does not vary dependent on the interest rate, while demand for money decreases the lower the interest rate as the opportunity cost of holding cash balances decreases. This results in an equilibrium being reached at an interest rate of r^*. You will study money markets in much more detail in the Macroeconomics component of the course.

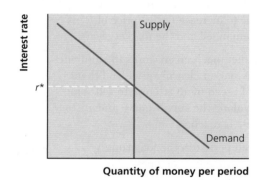

Figure 8 Money market equilibrium

Changes in the market equilibrium

Changes in the market equilibrium occur because of changes in the supply and demand for a product. This can happen as a result of any of the non-price factors that cause the supply or demand curves to shift, explained previously. For example, the decreased costs associated with running an online business resulting from technological advancements will have led to a decrease in the costs of production of a budget airline that uses the internet to sell tickets and interact with customers. As illustrated in Figure 9, this will cause the supply curve for budget airlines to shift to the right, as it is now more profitable to operate in this industry. This will cause the price of these flights to decrease from P_1 to P_2 and the equilibrium quantity to increase from Q_1 to Q_2.

Exam tip

Some questions will require you to shift both the supply and the demand curve, but do this only if there are clear changes in non-price determinants which affect both supply and demand mentioned in the case study.

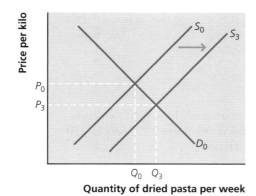

Figure 9 Increase in supply

Moreover, changes in one market can have an impact on related markets. Using our example of budget airlines, the decrease in the price of these flights could result in consumers switching away from traditional high street travel agents to booking their holidays online. This would result in the demand curve for traditional high street agents (a substitute) shifting to the left, which would result in the equilibrium price and quantity in this market falling. This could then have an effect on the labour market for travel agent workers, who would experience a decrease in the demand for their labour (and a subsequent decrease in their wage and employment levels) as a result of there being less demand for the product they produce. This demonstrates the knock-on effects which can explain why market equilibriums are constantly changing.

Some markets are often characterised by 'volatile' prices. This occurs in instances where, for whatever reason, supply and demand are likely to experience significant changes. Commodity markets are a good example of this – because the production of goods such as wheat is heavily dependent on the weather, supply is constantly fluctuating and thus, through the market mechanism, the price is changing regularly.

The model of supply and demand is extremely useful to economists in explaining how markets function. However, this does assume that there is no interference with resource allocation from the government. In reality, as we saw when discussing the impact of different economic systems, the government often intervenes in markets, resulting in outcomes that cannot be explained by the concept of supply and demand alone.

Elasticity

Price elasticity of demand (PED)

Price elasticity of demand measures the responsiveness of quantity demanded to a change in price. It can be calculated using the formula:

$$\text{PED} = \frac{\% \text{ change in quantity demanded}}{\% \text{ change in price}}$$

Knowledge check 11

How can the market mechanism be used to explain why the price of Easter eggs could be described as volatile?

Exam tip

Producing a definition using the equation rather than words is perfectly acceptable in the exam for any question that asks you to define one of the elasticities.

In the exam you will be required to calculate PED. When doing this, it is crucial that you know how to accurately calculate a percentage change. This can be done using the simple formula:

$$\frac{\text{new value} - \text{original value}}{\text{original value}} \times 100$$

Suppose the price of a chocolate bar in the school vending machine increases from 50p to 60p and that this causes the quantity demanded to fall from 250 bars to 230 bars. The price elasticity of demand can be found as follows:

% change in quantity demanded = $(230 - 250) \div 250 \times 100 = -8\%$

% change in price = $(60 - 50) \div 50 \times 100 = 20\%$

PED = $-8\% \div 20\%$ = **−0.4**

Given that the demand curve is downward sloping, the price elasticity of demand will always be negative – this is because an increase in price will result in a decrease in quantity demanded and a decrease in price will result in an increase in quantity demanded. Because PED is always negative, economists often ignore the minus sign when interpreting PED figures.

It is important to understand the difference between price elastic and price inelastic demand:

- *Price elastic demand* – quantity demanded responds more than proportionally to a change in price. This occurs when the PED is greater than one. In these instances we say demand is sensitive to changes in the price. For example, a PED of −1.4 would indicate that a 10% increase in the price would result in a 14% decrease in quantity demanded.
- *Price inelastic demand* – quantity demanded responds less than proportionally to a change in price. In these instances we say demand is insensitive to changes in the price. For example, a PED of −0.8 would indicate that a 10% increase in the price would result in an 8% decrease in quantity demanded.

These concepts are illustrated graphically in Figure 10.

> **Knowledge check 12**
>
> Based on the calculation made previously, is the demand for chocolate price elastic or inelastic? Is this what you would have expected?

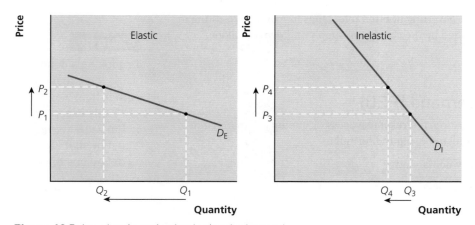

Figure 10 Price elastic and price inelastic demand

When demand is price elastic, a small increase in price from P_1 to P_2 will cause a significant decrease in quantity demanded from Q_1 to Q_2. When demand is price inelastic, a large increase in price from P_3 to P_4 will result in only a small decrease in quantity demanded from Q_3 to Q_4.

You also need to be aware of the concept of unit elastic demand, a special case in which the quantity demanded responds directly proportionally to a change in price. In this instance PED would be equal to $(-)1$, as a 10% increase in price would result in a 10% decrease in quantity demanded.

The price elasticity of demand varies along a straight-line demand curve, as illustrated in Figure 11. This is simple to understand when elasticities are based on percentage changes. When prices are high and quantity demanded is low, a large absolute change in price (say, for example, a chocolate bar increasing in price by £1) would not represent a large percentage change in price (if the price were already £15), while the absolute change in quantity demanded that results (say, for example, a 15-unit decrease in quantity demanded) represents a significant percentage change in quantity demanded (as quantity demanded was already low at, for example, 20 units). This would therefore result in demand being price elastic on this portion of the demand curve. The reverse is true at low prices, explaining why the demand curve is inelastic on this portion of the demand curve.

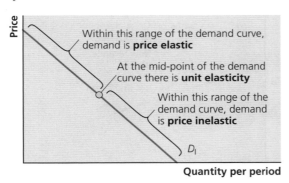

Figure 11 PED and the demand curve

Determinants of PED

The price elasticity of demand for a product is determined by a number of factors:

- *Availability of substitutes* – demand will be more price elastic when there are close substitutes available. For example, demand for a meal from a local fried chicken shop is likely to be price elastic, as a small increase in price will result in consumers switching away to consume chicken from a rival firm.
- *The nature of the good* – necessity goods are likely to have price inelastic demand as consumers will purchase similar quantities regardless of the price. Were oxygen sold in a market and not freely available, demand would be price inelastic as quantity demanded would not fall even if the price increased substantially. The reverse is true of luxury goods – as consumers can live without them, demand is likely to be price elastic.
- *Time period* – consumers' habits take time to change, meaning demand for most products becomes more price elastic in the long run.
- *Relative share of the good in overall expenditure* – consumers are less affected by changes in the price of goods and services that take up a low proportion of

their income, meaning demand for such goods tends to be more price inelastic. For example, even if the price of a chocolate bar increased by 50% from 50p to 75p, quantity demanded would be unlikely to fall by much as consumers are comfortably going to be able to afford the 25p increase in price.

The influence of PED on revenue

Businesses find the theory of price elasticity of demand useful in helping them understand how to change the price of their product in order to maximise total revenue.

Revenue = Price × Quantity

- When demand is price inelastic, firms should increase prices. This is because the decrease in quantity demanded will be smaller than the increase in price, as quantity demanded responds less than proportionally to a change in price, meaning revenue will increase.
- When demand is price elastic, firms should decrease prices. This is because the increase in quantity demanded will be greater than the decrease in price, as quantity demanded responds more than proportionally to a change in price, meaning revenue will increase.

Knowledge check 13

Why might a firm decide to decrease the price of its product even when demand is price inelastic?

This is illustrated in Figure 12.

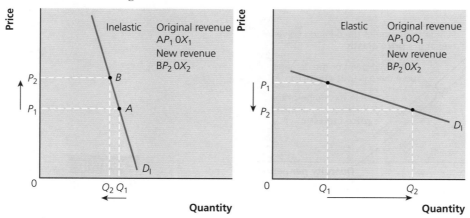

Figure 12 The influence of PED on revenue

Evaluating PED

While price elasticity of demand can be useful in helping firms determine prices, it has a number of limitations that must be considered:

- Elasticities are estimates which may be inaccurate. They are true only at one point in time based on sample data so may not be able to accurately predict what will happen when prices are changed.
- Ceteris paribus may not hold. If other non-price factors are changing when firms change the price of their product, PED will not be useful in predicting what will happen to quantity demanded.
- Estimates are valid for marginal price changes only. Because the price elasticity of demand changes as you move along the demand curve, these point estimates explain only what will happen to demand if prices are adjusted by a small amount.

Income elasticity of demand (YED)

Income elasticity of demand measures the responsiveness of quantity demanded to a change in income. It can be calculated using the formula:

$$YED = \frac{\% \text{ change in quantity demanded}}{\% \text{ change in income}}$$

As with price elasticity of demand, demand can be both income elastic and income inelastic:

- *Income elastic demand* – quantity demanded responds more than proportionally to a change in income. This occurs when the YED is greater than one.
- *Income inelastic demand* – quantity demanded responds less than proportionally to a change in income. This occurs when the YED is less than one.

Both the sign and size of the estimate help us categorise the good as shown in the table.

Type of good	Explanation	YED
Inferior	Quantity demanded decreases when income increases, as consumers switch away to better quality substitutes. An example would be the value range products in supermarkets	Negative
Necessity	Quantity demanded is unresponsive to changes in income. Demand for bread is unlikely to change much when income changes	Positive, close to zero
Normal	Quantity demanded increases when income increases. The demand for meat is likely to increase when income increases	Positive, between zero and one
Superior	Quantity demanded is very sensitive to changes in income. For example, when income increases there is likely to be a significant increase in demand for foreign holidays	Positive, greater than one

Evaluating YED

Income elasticity of demand can help firms estimate what will happen to their level of demand in the future, which is useful for forward planning.

However, the problem of these elasticities being estimates and ceteris paribus potentially not holding explained when critiquing PED also applies here and weakens YED's relevance to firms. Moreover, for these estimates to be of any use to firms they require accurate forecasts of future income to exist. Even if a firm has an accurate YED, future demand can be predicted only if firms know what will happen to consumer income in the future. Given that such macroeconomic predictions are notoriously difficult to make, this significantly weakens the value of income elasticity of demand estimates to firms.

Cross elasticity of demand (XED)

We know from the determinants of demand that the demand for one product is affected by changes in the price of another product. Cross elasticity of demand provides us with a numerical measure of the relationship between two goods.

Knowledge check 14

If demand for holidays to Spain is expected to increase from 145,000 to 159,000 next year when average incomes in an economy increase by 4%, calculate the income elasticity of demand.

Exam tip

It is important to bear in mind the estimated nature of YED figures before determining the type of good the estimate is describing. This is particularly true when the YED is close to a categorisation boundary. For example, a YED estimate for milk of −0.2 is more likely to suggest an estimation error than milk being an inferior good.

Cross elasticity of demand measures the responsiveness of quantity demanded of one good to a change in the price of another good. It can be calculated using the formula:

$$XED = \frac{\% \text{ change in quantity demanded of good X}}{\% \text{ change in price of good Y}}$$

As with all elasticities estimates, demand can be both cross elastic and cross inelastic:

- *Cross elastic demand* – quantity demanded of one product responds more than proportionally to a change in the price of another product. This occurs when the XED is greater than one.
- *Cross inelastic demand* – quantity demanded of one product responds less than proportionally to a change in the price of another product. This occurs when the XED is less than one.

The sign of the estimate helps us understand the relationship between the two goods:

- *Positive XED* – products are substitutes, as an increase in the price of one causes an increase in the demand for the other. Consumers switch away to consuming the now relatively cheaper product.
- *Negative XED* – products are complements, as an increase in the price of one causes a decrease in the demand for another. This is because the goods are in joint demand so an increase in the price of one increases the overall cost of consuming the goods and therefore reduces the demand for both of them.

Evaluating YED

Knowledge of cross elasticity of demand estimates can help firms understand how the demand for their products can be affected by what is happening in other markets. For example, if a firm is aware it has an XED of 1.4 with another product, it will pay close attention to the price of that product, knowing a 10% decrease in the price of that substitute would cause a 14% decrease in its own demand.

However, the estimated nature of these elasticities once again limits their value. It is important to remember that many products are entirely unrelated and that, while this should deliver an XED of zero, estimation errors mean the XED may lead us to draw the incorrect conclusion that such products are either complements or substitutes. This is why XED estimates are of limited use when they are close to zero. The further they are from zero, the greater the degree of substitutability (when XED is positive) or complementarity (when XED is negative).

Price elasticity of supply (PES)

Price elasticity of supply measures the responsiveness of quantity supplied to a change in price. It can be calculated using the formula:

$$PES = \frac{\% \text{ change in quantity supplied}}{\% \text{ change in price}}$$

Given that the supply curve is upward sloping, price elasticity of supply will always be positive – an increase in price will never cause the quantity supplied to decrease, as firms are able to make a greater profit when the price increases.

> **Knowledge check 15**
>
> Calculate and interpret the XED estimate when a decrease in the price of a laptop from £450 to £400 decreases the demand for tablet computers by 7%.

As with elasticities of demand, it is possible to categorise supply into being price elastic or price inelastic:

- *Price elastic supply* – quantity supplied responds more than proportionally to a change in price. This occurs when PES is greater than one.
- *Price inelastic supply* – quantity supplied responds less than proportionally to a change in price. This occurs when PES is less than one.

These concepts are illustrated in Figure 13. When supply is price elastic, a small increase in price from P_1 to P_2 will cause a significant increase in quantity supplied from Q_1 to Q_2. When supply is price inelastic, a large increase in price from P_3 to P_4 will result in only a small increase in quantity supplied from Q_3 to Q_4.

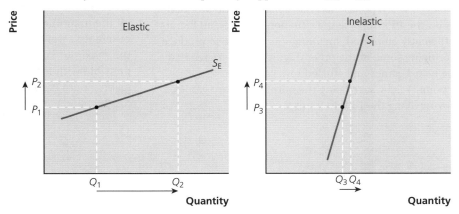

Figure 13 Price elastic and price inelastic supply

Knowledge check 16

Calculate the price elasticity of supply when an increase in the price of houses from £205,000 to £225,000 causes the quantity of houses built to increase from 105,000 to 108,000.

Determinants of PES

The price elasticity of supply for a product is determined by a number of factors:

- *Availability of stocks* – supply will be more price elastic for products that can be stored. Books, for example, have more elastic supply than eggs, as if the price of books falls it is possible to release supply from stock, which is not possible with eggs as they are perishable goods.
- *Available capacity* – firms will have inelastic supply when all of their resources are already employed; while they would like to increase supply when the price increases, they will not be able to because they have no spare capacity.
- *Time period* – supply tends to be more elastic in the long run when firms have a chance to respond to changes in the price. This is particularly true for products that take a long time to produce, for which it is not possible to alter supply in the short run.

It is important to be aware of a special case when supply is **perfectly inelastic**. In this instance, PES is equal to zero and the supply curve is a vertical straight line. This is likely to occur in markets where supply is fixed. An example would be tickets to a football match at Wembley Stadium, where the supply remains constant at 80,000 seats regardless of the price because the capacity of the stadium is fixed.

Perfectly inelastic
Quantity supplied is entirely unresponsive to changes in price.

Evaluating PES

Price elasticity of supply indicates to firms how responsive they are able to be to changes in market conditions. Firms would therefore desire a price elastic supply, as it enables them to profit from any changes in consumer demand, but this will not always be possible to achieve in all markets. In many ways, given that firms already know a lot about their own behaviour, elasticity of demand estimates that tell them about consumer behaviour are likely to be much more valuable to firms.

Productive and allocative efficiency

Productive efficiency

For **productive efficiency** to be achieved, a firm essentially has to be producing maximum output at the lowest possible cost. It is possible to explain each of these concepts using diagrams:

■ *Maximum output* – this is achieved when production takes place on the production possibility frontier. All points on the PPF represent a situation in which all factors of production are fully and efficiently employed, meaning it is possible to produce more of one good without sacrificing some of the other. Figure 14 illustrates that the only way a firm producing board games and stuffed toys can increase the production of stuffed toys at point A is by sacrificing the output of board games, which can be achieved by moving along the PPF to point B.

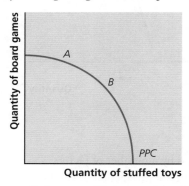

Figure 14 Opportunity cost and the PPF

■ *Lowest possible cost* – this is achieved when production takes place at the minimum efficient scale, i.e. where average costs are minimised. This is illustrated in Figure 15, with production taking place at Q*.

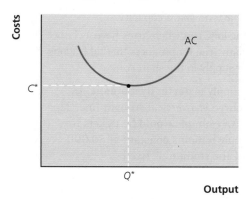

Figure 15 Production at the minimum efficient scale

Productive efficiency Production takes place where average costs are minimised (at the minimum efficient scale) and the maximum output possible with the given inputs is being produced.

Allocative efficiency

For **allocative efficiency** to be achieved, scarce resources have to be allocated in a way that best meets consumer preferences. The concept of the margin is important in understanding this type of efficiency.

We know from the study of consumer and producer surplus that not all firms derive the same benefit from consuming or producing a good. In Figure 16, consider resources being allocated in a way that results in Q_M units of output being produced. At a price of P_M, there is no incentive for consumers to enter or leave the market. This is because all consumers on the demand curve before Q_M are enjoying a positive consumer surplus and all consumers on the demand curve beyond Q_M value the good below the price. The key insight is that no consumer surplus is being made on the marginal unit – the marginal benefit is equal to the price.

Firms can be described in the same way at Q_M, where there is no incentive for firms to enter or leave the market. This is because all producers on the supply curve before Q_M enjoy producer surplus and all producers beyond Q_M see the cost of their production as being above the price. The key insight is that no producer surplus is being made on the marginal unit – the marginal cost of production is equal to the price.

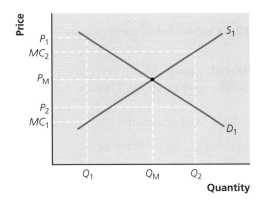

Figure 16 Allocative efficiency

We can explain why this is the allocative efficiency level of output by considering alternatives. Suppose output was at Q_1, with the price at P_1. At this level of output, it is clear to see that the marginal benefit enjoyed by consumers (P_1) is significantly greater than the marginal cost of firms producing the good (MC_1). This is an allocatively inefficient outcome – consumers value the good at a higher price than the cost of increasing output, meaning more scarce resources should be allocated to the production of this product. The reverse is true at Q_2, where the marginal benefit enjoyed by consumers (P_2) is significantly below the marginal cost producers incur from producing the good (MC_2). Society would therefore be better off if less scarce resources were allocated to the production of this product.

This thus gives us the important result that allocative efficiency occurs where price equals marginal cost and, therefore, the marginal benefit derived from consuming the good is equal to the marginal cost of producing it. When markets are working efficiently, then, allocative efficiency is achieved when supply equals demand.

Allocative efficiency
Where consumer satisfaction is maximised, which occurs when price equals marginal cost ($P = MC$).

Exam tip

Markets fail when they are unable to achieve an allocatively efficient outcome for society – it is in these instances that the government intervenes in an attempt to overcome market failure.

Economic efficiency

Economic efficiency describes a situation in which both productive and allocative efficiency is being achieved. Resources are not only being employed efficiently to produce maximum output at the lowest cost, they are also being allocated to produce goods and services most desired by consumers.

When exploring the role of economists in allocating resources, we said three fundamental questions had to be answered: what to produce, how to produce and for whom to produce?

These efficiencies provide answers to two of these questions. Allocative efficiency indicates what needs to be produced and productive efficiency indicates how this production should take place. However, they fail to answer the final, and perhaps most complex, question: how should this production be distributed among the population? The concept of equity – fairness – is important here. Economies may well be productively and allocatively efficient but still fail to deliver the best outcome for society if resources are heavily concentrated in the hands of a few wealthy citizens. The government is therefore faced with a difficult task of achieving equity, which often conflicts with efficiency objectives.

Costs and revenue

The *total cost (TC)* incurred by a firm when producing a given level of output can be calculated by:

Total cost (TC) = Total fixed cost (TFC) + Total variable cost (TVC)

- *Total fixed cost (TFC)* – costs that do not vary with the level of output. They are often known as sunk costs.
- *Total variable cost (TVC)* – costs that increase with the level of output.

Average total cost (ATC or AC) represents the cost per unit of output. It can be calculated by:

$$\frac{\text{Total cost (TC)}}{\text{Output}}$$

Marginal cost (MC) represents the change in total cost as a result of increasing output by one unit.

Economies and diseconomies of scale

Economies of scale chart the relationship between the level of output (of either a firm or an industry) and a firm's long run average costs.

Internal economies and diseconomies of scale

Internal economies of scale refer to a reduction in a firm's long run average costs as a result of an increase in its level of output. This is illustrated in Figure 17, where an increase in the level of output from Q_1 to Q_2 results in a decrease in the firm's long run average costs from C_1 to C_2. There are a number of reasons why this may happen:

- *Purchasing economies* – larger firms bulk buy their inputs. Because they are a more important customer to the supplier they are able to negotiate discounts on these inputs.

Knowledge check 17

Assume there are only two costs involved in operating a pen factory – renting the factory and buying the ink for the pens. The cost of producing 100,000 pens is £40,000. Which costs are fixed and which are variable? Calculate the average cost.

- *Selling economies* – large firms can make fuller use of sales and distribution facilities than a small firm. For example, it does not cost double the price to transport double the amount of output to a consumer (while a larger vehicle may require more fuel, the driver will be paid a similar wage).
- *Technical economies* – large firms find it cost-efficient to use technology, as they can spread the cost of this often expensive technology over a large volume of output.

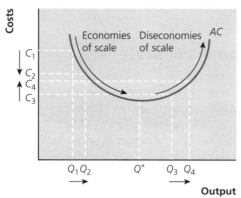

Figure 17 Internal economies of scale

- *Managerial economies* – as firms grow, they employ a larger workforce, which enables them to benefit from specialisation resulting from the division of labour.
- *Financial economies* – because larger firms have more assets, they are able to borrow at lower interest rates.
- *Risk-bearing economies* – large firms can diversify their output, which enables them to limit their risk.

However, when a firm grows too large, it can begin to experience internal diseconomies of scale. This is when a firm's long run average costs increase as a result of an increase in its level of output. The right-hand portion of the average cost curve in Figure 17 illustrates this concept, where an increase in the level of output from Q_3 to Q_4 results in an increase in the firm's long run average costs from C_3 to C_4. There are a number of reasons why this might happen:

- *Coordination problems* – larger firms find it more difficult to coordinate production, meaning inefficiencies can start to develop. For example, a large airline operating hundreds of flights a day will find it difficult to effectively monitor the efficiency of its thousands of check-in desks around the world to see whether any cost savings can be made.
- *Slows decision making* – as firms grow, their chain of command tends to increase; the slower decision making that results from this can make businesses less responsive to market conditions and raise their costs as a consequence.
- *Worsened industrial relations* – those who work for large employers often feel undervalued, believing they are not making a significant contribution to the performance of the firm. Such workers tend to be less motivated and are therefore less productive as a consequence.

Firms producing at the lowest attainable average cost are said to be operating at the **minimum efficient scale**. This is illustrated by the output level Q^* in Figure 17. Firms are said to be productively efficient when producing at this level.

Knowledge check 18

Explain three examples of economies of scale a large supermarket is likely to benefit from.

Knowledge check 19

Explain, with examples, why slower decision making may represent a diseconomy of scale experienced by a large supermarket.

Minimum efficient scale
Total long run average costs are minimised and all internal economies of scale are being taken advantage of.

In competitive markets, utilising internal economies of scale can be essential in enabling a firm to compete successfully. After all, a firm with lower costs is able to charge lower prices and therefore increase its market share. However, the importance of economies of scale does depend on the nature of the industry. In some instances, often in markets that do not involve expensive technology and require a significant amount of personalised customer interaction, the minimum efficient scale actually occurs at a very low level of output. In such instances being large is of little advantage to a firm.

External economies and diseconomies of scale

External economies of scale refer to a reduction in a firm's long run average costs as a result of the growth of industry output. This is illustrated in Figure 18, where an increase in industry output could cause the long run average cost curve to shift downwards from AC_1 to AC_2, resulting in a firm's costs falling from C_1 to C_2. The idea that a firm can experience falling costs when its own level of output is unchanged simply as a result of industry output increasing can be explained in a number of ways:

- *Skilled labour* – when the industry grows, more individuals seek out their own training in the industry because they believe there will be good job opportunities in the future. This means firms have access to a larger pool of skilled labour.
- *Ancillary economies* – when there are more firms in the industry there may be an increase in the number of ancillary firms that provide inputs, as such firms realise they will experience more demand. This can improve competition in the input market and lead to lower input prices for firms.
- *Specialisation* – when the industry grows, demand may be high enough for individual firms to become more specialised in a segment of the industry, which can decrease their long run average costs as they sell the same volume of output over a narrower product range.

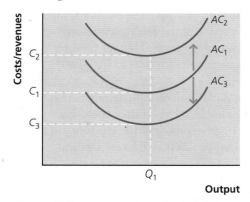

Figure 18 External economies of scale

Knowledge check 20

How might the reputation of an individual firm be enhanced when an industry grows? How does this link to the concept of external economies of scale?

However, growth in the size of the industry can also generate external diseconomies of scale, where a firm's long run average costs increase as a result of the growth of industry output. There is one primary explanation for this: when there are more firms in the market, there is more competition for inputs, which can drive up the cost of these and therefore result in higher long run average costs. This is particularly true in industries where firms rely on scarce natural resources to produce their products.

Summary

After studying the topic of *How competitive markets work* you should be able to:

- Discuss the role incentives have on the behaviour of different economic agents in allocating resources.
- Appreciate the different economic systems that exist to allocate resources in an economy.
- Understand what causes movements along and shifts of supply and demand curves.
- Evaluate the impact of changes in the price on consumer and producer surplus.
- Understand how market equilibrium is determined and evaluate the consequences of disequilibrium in a market.
- Discuss the impact of changes in demand and supply on the market equilibrium using a demand and supply diagram.

- Calculate and interpret price elasticity of demand, income elasticity of demand, cross elasticity of demand and price elasticity of supply estimates.
- Illustrate the impact price elasticity of demand has on a firm's revenue when making pricing decisions.
- Discuss the usefulness and significance of elasticities to economic agents.
- Explain what is meant by productive, allocative and economic efficiency.
- Understand and calculate total cost, total fixed cost, total variable cost, average cost, average fixed cost and marginal cost.
- Discuss the causes and consequences of internal and external economies and diseconomies of scale.

■ Market failure and government intervention

Market failure

Market failure occurs when the market mechanism leads to a sub-optimal allocation of resources. When supply and demand do not accurately reflect the true costs and benefits involved in producing or consuming a particular good, allocative efficiency will result when resource allocation is left to the free market. This is because the marginal social cost (MSC) – the cost to society of producing an extra unit of output – will not be equal to the marginal social benefit (MSB), which is the additional benefit that society gains from consuming an extra unit of a good.

This can result in a situation of under- or over-production or consumption. For example, suppose the market mechanism results in an equilibrium in which the marginal social cost of production exceeds the marginal social benefit. The market is failing here because too many scarce resources are being allocated to the production of this product; social welfare would be improved if production were to fall.

There are three main causes of market failure studied in this unit:
- Public goods
- Externalities
- Information asymmetries

> **Knowledge check 21**
>
> Why would a situation in which the MSB of consuming a good exceeded the MSC represent market failure?

Public goods

Public goods are defined as being non-excludable and non-rival:

- *Non-excludable* – once provided, individuals cannot be excluded from consuming the good.
- *Non-rival* – consumption of the good by one person does not prevent someone else from consuming the good.

Street lights are perhaps the most famous example of a public good. Once provided, it would be very difficult, if not impossible, to stop anyone benefiting from their consumption – anyone walking down the street would benefit from their presence. Moreover, the ability for an individual to benefit from the light is not affected by the number of other individuals who have previously benefited from the light by walking down the street.

Public goods create a free-rider problem. Because of the non-rival and non-excludable nature of the goods, individuals will not be willing to pay for them, knowing they can 'free-ride' and enjoy the benefits of consumption without paying. This can therefore result in a situation of what is known as 'missing markets' – because individuals have no incentive to pay for the goods, there is a risk that they will not be provided in a free market.

The government therefore has an important role to play in the provision of public goods. Such goods are often funded out of tax revenue, and while they may be provided by private companies, they tend to be supported by government funding. Of course, the extent of government provision is likely to depend on the extent to which it is possible to overcome the free-rider problem by finding ways to make the good excludable or chargeable and how large the opportunity cost of such provision is.

Exam tip
Few goods can be described as being entirely non-rival and non-excludable. Those with elements of non-rivalry and non-excludability are known as quasi-public goods.

Externalities

The private costs and benefits experienced by individuals and firms determine the equilibrium reached in the market mechanism.

- The demand curve can be translated into the marginal private benefit curve – each point on the demand curve represents the benefit to the individual of consuming an extra unit of the good.
- The supply curve can be translated into the marginal private cost curve – each point on the supply curve represents the cost to firms of producing an extra unit of the good.

In some markets, the production or consumption of a product results in individuals or firms outside of the market transaction experiencing benefits or costs. Such agents are known as **third parties**. The benefits or costs these individuals incur are known as the marginal external costs and benefits of production or consumption. These are referred to as externalities. Social costs or benefits are, of course, the total costs or benefits to society of the consumption or production of a good or service:

- Marginal social cost = Marginal private cost + marginal external cost
- Marginal social benefit = Marginal private benefit + marginal external benefit

In instances where externalities exist, markets fail. Consumers and producers consider only their own costs and benefits when making consumption and production decisions, meaning external costs and benefits are ignored. This divergence between

Third parties
Individuals or firms that have no input into the market transaction but are affected by its outcome.

social and private costs and benefits generates a market equilibrium where marginal social benefit is not equal to marginal private benefit, meaning markets fail to achieve allocative efficiency.

Negative externalities of consumption

Negative externalities of consumption occur when third parties outside of the market transaction are harmed by the consumption of a good or service. Take the example of cigarettes. Individuals who smoke do so because they derive a private benefit from the activity. However, the action can cause harm to third parties, such as those in the same room as the smoker, who suffer from passive smoking. This results in the marginal private benefit (MPB) of smoking exceeding the marginal social benefit (MSB) of smoking, as illustrated in Figure 19.

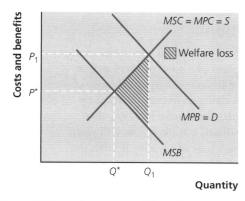

Figure 19 Negative externalities of consumption

The market equilibrium occurs where supply equals demand (when MPB = MPC). This will create a problem of over-consumption. Q_1 cigarettes will be consumed, which exceeds the socially optimal level of consumption at Q^*. This over-consumption occurs because individuals ignore the harm to third parties when deciding how many cigarettes to consume. This creates a situation of allocative efficiency and a welfare loss of the shaded region – for all units of consumption between Q^* and Q_1, the marginal social cost of consumption exceeds the marginal social benefit.

Negative externalities of production

Negative externalities of production occur when third parties outside of the market transaction are harmed by the production of a good or service. The production that takes place in many factories generates negative externalities. This is because the production process incurs private costs not only to firms (in the form of purchasing their inputs and running the factory) but also to third parties, such as local residents, who are harmed by the toxic fumes emitted from the factory, and more broadly the whole of society, which is harmed by global warming. The result is that the marginal social cost of production exceeds the marginal private cost, as illustrated in Figure 20.

This generates a problem of over-production. Q_1 units of output will be produced by the factory, which exceeds the socially optimal level of production of Q^*. This occurs because firms only consider their own private costs when making production decisions. Allocative inefficiency and a welfare loss of the shaded region result.

Knowledge check 22

Why might alcohol be seen to generate negative externalities of consumption?

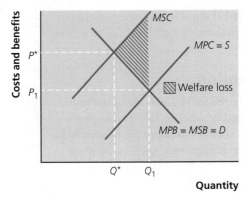

Figure 20 Negative externalities of production

Positive externalities of consumption

Positive externalities of consumption occur when third parties outside of the market transaction benefit from other individuals' consumption of a good or service. For example, you are most likely revising for your A-level Economics exam because of the private benefits you believe you will derive from doing so in the future, such as a highly paid or satisfying job. However, your consumption of education also generates positive externalities – by being more qualified, it is likely you will earn a higher income in the future, which will benefit the whole of society through the higher income tax you are likely to pay. This results in the marginal social benefit of consumption exceeding the marginal private benefit, as illustrated in Figure 21.

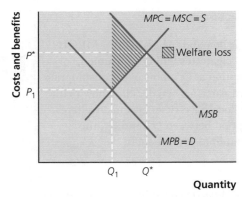

Figure 21 Positive externalities of consumption

Under-consumption results if education is left to the free market, where individuals are required to pay for the education they receive. Society would benefit if $(Q^* - Q_1)$ more individuals purchased education, but this does not happen because individuals ignore third-party benefits.

Positive externalities of production

Positive externalities of production occur when third parties outside of the market transaction benefit from other firms' production of a good or service. Take the example of a firm investing heavily in research and development. The firm is likely to experience very high private costs. However, should its research result in a technological breakthrough, this will reduce the costs of many other firms which will be able to benefit from this technology. This means the marginal private cost of this investment is higher than the marginal social cost, as illustrated in Figure 22.

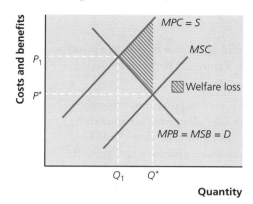

Figure 22 Positive externalities of production

In the free market there will be under-investment in research and development. This under-production results because firms do not consider the benefits to other firms which will result from their efforts when making the decision about how much to spend on research and development. The result is that allocative efficiency will occur; the marginal social benefit from undertaking more research and development would exceed the marginal social cost.

Information asymmetries

Information failure occurs when economic agents do not have perfect knowledge – a lack of information means they make decisions that do not maximise their welfare. As well as the problems associated with merit and demerit goods, there are two other causes of information failure:

- *Asymmetric information* – a situation in which information is not shared equally between parties in a market transaction. An example of when this could cause a problem is in the private healthcare market. There is asymmetric information because doctors know far more than their patients about medical conditions. In a free market where producers are motivated by profit it would be possible for a doctor to abuse this information asymmetry by prescribing patients expensive medication they do not need – a patient is likely to be willing to consume it, but only because they lack the information that they do not really require the medication.
- *Moral hazard* – a situation in which a person who has taken out insurance is prone to taking more risk. An example here is with mobile phone insurance – because this has transferred the burden of risk, individuals with insurance are likely to take less care over their phone, increasing the probability of them losing or damaging it.

Merit goods

Merit goods are goods that are more beneficial to consumers than they realise. An example could be going to the gym. Because individuals are myopic (thinking only about the present), when deciding whether to consume the good they may consider

Knowledge check 23

How can the concept of asymmetric information be applied to the market for second-hand cars?

simply the immediate physical and emotional benefits that result from exercise. They may therefore not be considering the future benefits they will enjoy from going to the gym, such as increased life expectancy. The argument here is that it will create a situation in which the marginal social benefit exceeds the marginal private benefit, as society believes consumption will bring individuals more benefits than they realise. This creates a situation of under-consumption.

We can draw comparisons with the outcome in a merit good case to that in a positive externalities of consumption case by looking back at Figure 21; both are modelled identically.

When evaluating the significance of merit goods, it is very important to remember that there are normative value judgements involved in deciding whether something is a merit good. For example, some argue the opera is a merit good that would be under-consumed in the free market because individuals are unable to recognise the true benefits they derive from visiting the opera. This is clearly something which is debatable and cannot be proven.

Demerit goods

Demerit goods are good that bring less benefit to consumers than they expect. An example could be addictive drugs. Consumers may well over-value the benefits they derive from consumption, failing to think about the harm such drug use can cause, such as serious damage to their health. The argument here is that market failure will result because the marginal private benefit of consumption exceeds the marginal social benefit – society believes the consumption of the good will bring less benefit to individuals than they believe to be the case. Parallels can be drawn between this case and that of negative externalities of consumption – looking back at Figure 19, we can see that both would be modelled identically. In both cases, there is allocative inefficiency generated by an over-consumption problem.

Some economists argue that the significance of demerit goods is diminishing over time as a result of increasingly knowledgeable consumers. The internet has significantly reduced the amount of information failure, as has a generally improved awareness of prevalent health issues. This could be used to argue that individuals who consume drugs are fully aware of the costs and benefits of doing so.

Alternative methods of government intervention

Taxation

An indirect tax is a tax levied on goods and services paid by producers to the government. Imposing an indirect tax will increase a producer's costs of production, decreasing the profitability of producing a good. As illustrated in Figure 23, this will cause the supply curve to shift to the left and result in the equilibrium quantity falling from Q_1 to Q_2.

This will be effective in overcoming market failure which results in over-consumption or over-production, as it will reduce the amount of production or consumption. In the case of negative externalities of production, some argue a tax is particularly effective as the negative externalities are internalised – firms now have to pay for the harm their production is causing third parties.

> **Exam tip**
>
> While merit goods and positive externalities of consumption can be represented on the same diagram, the policy solutions required to overcome the market failure they cause can be different. You therefore need to make sure you don't confuse externalities and information failure in the exam.

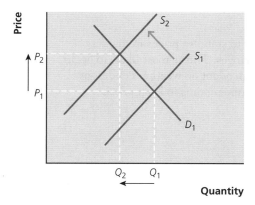

Figure 23 The effect of imposing an indirect tax

Subsidies

A subsidy is a payment by the government to a firm in order to incentivise production. This will decrease a firm's costs of production and cause the supply curve to shift to the right, as illustrated in Figure 24.

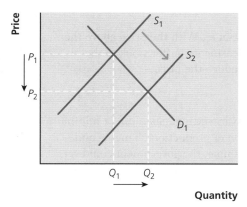

Figure 24 The effect of imposing a subsidy

The result will be an increase in equilibrium quantity, meaning this will help overcome market failure associated with under-consumption or under-production. The problem with subsidies, however, is that it is difficult to know how large a subsidy to impose because it is hard to estimate the size of the market failure.

State provision

By providing the good for free, consumption of the good will inevitably increase significantly, therefore proving very effective in overcoming any under-consumption that exists. However, such provision is clearly extremely costly and often incurs significant opportunity cost. The government is therefore likely to implement such a solution only in instances where it considers the market failure to be substantial. Even in instances where it does do this, such as health and education, consumers often abuse the free nature of the service and create significant inefficiency – for example, every year millions of pounds are wasted through patients failing to attend appointments they have made to see their GP.

Buffer stock systems

The government implements buffer stock schemes to stabilise prices in markets that are vulnerable to particularly volatile price changes. This is most likely to occur in agricultural markets, where supply is heavily dependent on weather conditions. Figure 25 illustrates a situation in which the government aims to keep prices stabilised between a floor and a ceiling price.

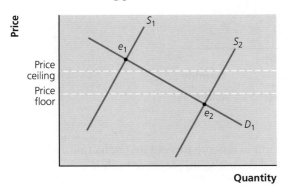

Figure 25 Buffer stock system

Suppose a bad harvest caused the market to operate at e_1. With the price above the price ceiling the government could intervene by releasing its buffer stock to the market, which would shift supply to the right and reduce the price.

Price controls

The government could intervene directly in markets by setting maximum or minimum prices. This could result in equilibrium consumption or production changing and therefore act as a solution to market failure. For example, the government could set a minimum price for a packet of cigarettes above the market equilibrium price, as illustrated in Figure 26.

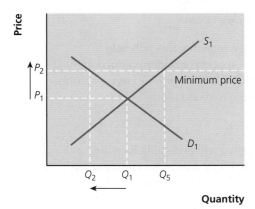

Figure 26 The effect of price controls

> ### Knowledge check 25
>
> Explain how the government would intervene in a situation where the price fell below the floor price, as illustrated by equilibrium e_2 in Figure 25.

Because consumers will respond to an increase in price by reducing their level of demand, this could effectively solve the over-consumption problem that occurs in the market for cigarettes. However, this assumes that demand is responsive to changes in the price. In reality, demand for addictive products such as cigarettes is price inelastic, rendering this policy ineffective. Moreover, because it will incentivise producers to increase their supply of cigarettes (to Q_s), it could result in black markets forming.

Legislation and regulation

The government intervenes in some markets by imposing a series of rules designed to correct market failure. In the most extreme cases this intervention can take the form of an outright ban. An example of this is in the market for many drugs the government has outlawed. This is obviously very effective in reducing consumption but can create problems with enforcement.

In other cases government rules often serve to increase a firm's costs of production. An example of this would be forcing firms to abide by a set of environmental standards. This would cause the supply curve to shift to the left and result in the production of a good falling.

Information provision

In the case of merit and demerit goods, the market failure arises because individuals are unable to accurately estimate the benefits they derive from consumption. Therefore, the government may intervene by improving the information in the market to increase individuals' awareness and change their levels of demand. An example of this would be in the market for fruit and vegetables, where the government has invested in advertising campaigns to promote the 'five a day' message, designed to increase the consumption of this merit good.

Whether this is an effective solution depends upon whether the information provision is well targeted and actually changes the behaviour of individuals. While warnings on the front of cigarette packets have led to a decrease in the number of people smoking in recent years, the reality is that many smokers ignore this information.

Government failure

Government failure occurs when government intervention in a market results in a misallocation of resources. It can be seen as a situation in which the government intervenes in a market to overcome market failure and ends up making the market even more allocatively inefficient.

There are several reasons why this can happen:

- *Difficulty in estimating market failure* – the government often has to act on partial information about what the market failure is, meaning the solution it implements may not solve the problem.
- *Lack of incentives* – where the government intervenes by providing the good, inefficiency often results because of the lack of the profit motive in the public sector.
- *Political interference* – much government policy is constrained or determined by the desire of governments to please their electorate.

> **Exam tip**
>
> Information provision will be ineffective in overcoming the market failure caused by externalities because informing individuals or firms about the benefits or costs incurred by third parties will not change their behaviour – they act as they do not because they are unaware of the impact on third parties but because they don't care as it does not affect their welfare.

Government failure can perhaps be limited by initiating clear target setting and in some instances introducing competition within state-controlled markets to improve efficiency. Given the risk of government failure, it could be said that the government should intervene only in instances of substantial market failure; it is in these circumstances where the government is least at risk of producing a worse outcome than the market would deliver.

Summary

After studying the topic of *Market failure and government intervention* you should be able to:

- Understand what is meant by market failure.
- Identify the characteristics of a public good and discuss the role of the government in providing such goods.
- Explain, using cost/benefit diagrams, how positive and negative externalities of consumption and production result in market failure.
- Understand what is meant by information failure, including the concepts of asymmetric information and moral hazard.
- Explain what is meant by merit and demerit goods and using cost/benefit diagrams evaluate the extent to which they result in market failure.
- Discuss the relative merits of the different government policies to solve market failure – taxation and subsidies, state provision, buffer stock schemes, price controls, legislation and regulation and information provision.
- Evaluate the causes and consequences of government failure.

Questions & Answers

This section provides an explanation of the structure of both the AS and A-level microeconomics papers and strategies for approaching the different types of questions you will encounter in the exam. This is followed by a series of sample questions covering all the question types – multiple-choice, data response and essays. After all of these questions there are some example answers from students. You should practise all of these questions yourself and compare your answers to these while reading the detailed exam advice to improve your understanding of what is required to achieve full marks.

Assessment objectives

To succeed in this course you will need to be able to demonstrate your ability in the following assessment objectives:

AO	Key skill	Explanation	Weighting at AS	Weighting at A-level
1	Knowledge	Demonstrate knowledge of terms/concepts and theories/models.	30%	22.5%
2	Application	Apply knowledge and understanding to various economic contexts.	30%	25%
3	Analysis	Analyse issues within economics, showing an understanding of their impact on economic agents.	20%	25%
4	Evaluation	Evaluate economic arguments and use qualitative and quantitative evidence to support informed judgements relating to economic issues.	20%	27.5%

AS microeconomics

This is examined by a 90-minute paper. There are 60 marks awarded for the paper; you therefore have approximately 90 seconds to answer each question.

The paper is split into three sections:

- **Section A – Multiple-choice**

    You will be asked 15 multiple-choice questions covering the AS microeconomics specification. These could require you to conduct simple calculations, interpret points on diagrams or recall knowledge about technical theory.

    Each question is worth 1 mark and you will have to select the correct answer from a choice of four options.

    You should aim to spend approximately 20 minutes on this section.

- **Section B – Data response**

    You will be presented with an extract giving you information about a particular market. You will then be asked a series of questions related to this market, which tests the full range of assessment objectives. Questions will range in value from straightforward 1-mark questions to a 10-mark question, which is level marked in the same way as the essays.

The section is worth a total of 25 marks and you should aim to spend approximately 40 minutes on it.

■ **Section C – Quantitative essay questions**

You will be given a choice of two essay questions and must answer one of these. The answer will require you to demonstrate some quantitative skills, most likely through drawing a diagram.

The essay is worth 20 marks and you should aim to spend approximately 30 minutes on it.

A-level microeconomics

This is examined by a 120-minute paper. There are 80 marks awarded for the paper; you therefore have approximately 90 seconds to answer each question.

The content covered in the paper will include everything in this book alongside the Year 2 microeconomics content.

The paper is split into three sections:

■ **Section A – Data response**

You will be given a variety of stimulus material, which is most likely to focus on a particular market. You will then be asked a series of questions related to this market, which tests the full range of assessment objectives. Questions will range in value from straightforward 2-mark questions to an 8- and a 12-mark question, both of which are level marked in the same way as the essays.

The section is worth a total of 30 marks and you should aim to spend approximately 40 minutes on it.

■ **Section B – Quantitative essay questions**

You will be given a choice of two essay questions and must answer one of these. The answer will require you to demonstrate some quantitative skills, most likely through drawing a diagram.

The essay is worth 25 marks and you should aim to spend approximately 40 minutes on it.

■ **Section C – Qualitative essay questions**

You will be given a choice of two essay questions and must answer one of these. These essays will not require you to demonstrate any quantitative skills but you may well find a diagram will support your discussion; relevant diagrams will be credited.

The essay is worth 25 marks and you should aim to spend approximately 40 minutes on it.

Answering multiple-choice questions

When answering multiple-choice questions you should do the following:

■ Work through them quickly – remember, you have only 90 seconds on average to complete each one. Some will take longer than this, but that should be compensated by others that are much quicker to complete. Do not spend too long on any one question.

- Cover up the options when reading the question and see whether you can work out the answer before looking at the four options – this is often quicker than reading the options and getting distracted by those that are incorrect but are close to being right.
- If unsure, eliminate those answers you know to be incorrect and choose between any options you have left – there is no penalty for answering incorrectly, so you should never leave an answer blank.
- When practising multiple-choice questions in the build-up to the exam, try to justify why the incorrect options are incorrect. This is done in the example multiple-choice questions in this guide.

Answering data-response questions

When answering data-response questions you should:

- Read the stimulus material very carefully, remembering to refer to it in your answers when required.
- Work out which assessment objectives the question is testing – do not waste time evaluating when the question is only asking to you offer an explanation.
- Make sure you always fully apply your answer to the market in the question; avoid producing theoretical answers that ignore the specifics given in the case study.

Answering essay questions

The most important thing to remember when answering essay questions is to cover each of the four skills tested by the assessment objectives. These essays, along with any questions that require evaluation in the data-response section, are level marked. Which level your answer is placed in depends upon how well you have covered each of the four skills – these are graded as being 'Limited', 'Reasonable', 'Good' or 'Strong'. Aim to get into the Strong category on all skills, as detailed in the table.

	AO1 and AO2	AO3	AO4
Limited	Awareness of the meaning of the terms in the question.	Simple statement(s) of cause and effect.	An unsupported assertion.
Reasonable	As above + applied to the context of the question.	An explanation of causes and consequences, which omits some key links in the chain of argument.	Some attempt to come to a conclusion, which shows some recognition of influencing factors.
Good	Precision in the use of the terms in the question and applied in a focused way to the context of the question.	An explanation of causes and consequences, developing most of the links in the chain of argument.	A conclusion is drawn weighing up both sides, but without reaching a supported judgement.
Strong		An explanation of causes and consequences, fully developing the links in the chain of argument.	A conclusion is drawn weighing up both sides, and reaches a supported judgement.

Generally, the best way to approach these questions is to fully analyse one side of the argument, analyse the other side and then reach a judgement saying which side of the argument is stronger and why you have reached this conclusion. This is likely to include a consideration of the factors your judgement depends upon.

■AS microeconomics Section A

Multiple-choice questions

Question 1

Which of the following represents a positive economic statement?

A   Tax increases are a more effective way of reducing the budget deficit than cutting benefits

B   On average, male workers earn more than female workers

C   Command economies lead to a fairer outcome for citizens of a country

D   Negative economic growth is more harmful to an economy than a balance of payments deficit

Question 2

Point X on the diagram below can best be described as being:

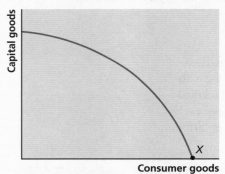

A   Allocatively efficient

B   Allocatively inefficient

C   Productively efficient

D   Productively inefficient

Question 3

The diagram below illustrates market failure occurring in the case of:

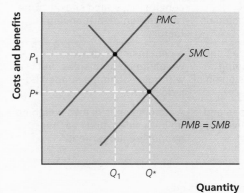

A   Merit goods

B   Negative externalities of consumption

C   Negative externalities of production

D   Positive externalities of production

Question 4

The income elasticity of demand for a product is estimated to be −1.2. This suggests that:

A   Demand is income-elastic and the product is an inferior good

B   Demand is income-inelastic and the product is an inferior good

C   Demand is income-elastic and the product is a luxury good

D   Demand is income-inelastic and the product is a luxury good

Question 5

Which of the following is the correct definition of external diseconomies of scale?

A   Decrease in long run average costs as a result of a firm increasing its level of output

B   Increase in long run average costs as a result of a firm increasing its level of output

C   Decrease in long run average costs as a result of an increase in the output of an industry

D   Increase in long run average costs as a result of an increase in the output of an industry

Question 6

Which of the following is not a common feature of a command economy?

A   Centrally determined prices

B   Shortages

C   Competition

D   Lack of entrepreneurship

Question 7

A corner shop raises the price of a bottle of milk from 75p to 82p. Demand for the milk falls from 300 bottles a week to 248 bottles as a result of this. Calculate the price elasticity of demand for milk.

A   −1.86

B   −0.54

C   2.25

D   −2.46

Question 8

Which of the following correctly identifies a public good?

A   Rival and excludable

B   Non-rival and excludable

C   Rival and non-excludable

D   Non-excludable and non-rival

Question 9

A merit goods case is a situation in which:

A   There is under-consumption because individuals under-value the external benefits of consuming the good

B   There is under-consumption because individuals under-value the private benefits of consuming the good

C   There is over-consumption because individuals under-value the external benefits of consuming the good

D   There is over-consumption because individuals under-value the private benefits of consuming the good

Question 10

An information campaign highlighting the damage caused to an individual's health from consuming a product would be an effective solution to the market failure resulting from:

A   Positive externalities

B   Negative externalities

C   Merit goods

D   Demerit goods

Answers and rationale

Question 1

A   This is impossible to test without knowing the proposed size of the tax increases and benefit cuts. Even if we did have this information the phrase 'more effective' is still subjective – this cannot even be taken to mean which policy will reduce the deficit by the biggest amount, as some would argue there are social concerns that need to be taken into account when making a judgement about effectiveness.

B   *Correct answer.* This could easily be proven true or false as there are objective data detailing the earnings of men and women.

C   The word 'fairer' is subjective – it is impossible to quantitatively measure fairness, as there are many different interpretations of what fairness means.

D   There is no accepted way to measure 'harm', meaning it is down to opinion which of these problems is more harmful to an economy.

Question2

A   The PPF tells us nothing about allocative efficiency because it does not give any indication about consumer preferences – we therefore do not know which point will represent the most efficient allocation of resources.

B   See above.

C   *Correct answer.* All points on the PPF are productively efficient, as all factors of production are fully and efficiently employed and there is an opportunity cost involved in increasing the output of capital goods – consumer goods would have to be sacrificed.

D   Do not fall into the trap of assuming that because no capital goods are being produced there must be productive inefficiency. Productive efficiency is not about whether the right combination of goods is being produced but whether this production is taking place making the least use of scarce resources possible.

Question 3

A   This occurs when individuals are not fully aware of the private benefits of consumption, so would be represented by demand being below the optimal level – there would be under-consumption.

B   In this instance PMB would be greater than SMB – there would be over-consumption.

C   SMC would be greater than PMC – there would be over-production.

D   *Correct answer.* Because of benefits to third parties that derive from the production of the good, social costs are lower than private costs, meaning there is under-production in the free market.

Question 4

A *Correct answer.* When YED is negative the product is an inferior good – an increase in income causes a decrease in the demand for the product. When YED is a number greater than one or less than minus one quantity demanded responds more than proportionally to a change in income, so demand is income elastic.

B Demand is not income-inelastic as quantity demanded responds more than proportionally to a change in income – a 10% decrease in income would cause a 12% increase in quantity demanded.

C The product is not a luxury good as YED is negative – luxury goods would have a positive YED as demand rises when income rises.

D The product is not a luxury good as YED would be positive for a luxury good and demand is not income-inelastic as quantity demanded responds more than proportionally to a change in income when YED = –1.2.

Question 5

A This is defining internal economies of scale.

B This is defining internal diseconomies of scale.

C This is defining external economies of scale.

D *Correct answer.*

Question 6

A In a command economy prices are not determined by the forces of supply and demand but are instead set at a level determined by central planning boards.

B Because there is no price mechanism to ensure markets clear in command economies, the price for some goods (often staple items) is set below the market equilibrium. This creates a situation of excess demand, meaning some people who are willing to pay the price of the good are left without the product. These shortages are sustained because there is no ability for the price to adjust to clear the shortage.

C *Correct answer.* In a command economy the government owns and allocates all resources – this means there are no private firms competing on price and quality for consumers, as the government provides all goods and services.

D In a command economy there is no profit incentive, as all firms are owned by the government. This means there tends to be a lack of entrepreneurship, as there is no incentive for private individuals and firms to be innovative or take risks because there is no reward available for doing so.

Question 7

A   Correct answer.
   % change in quantity demanded = (248 – 300) ÷ 300 × 100 = –17.3%
   % change in price = (82p – 75p) ÷ 75p × 100 = 9.3%
   PED = –17.3% ÷ 9.3% = –1.86

B   This answer is arrived at by getting the equation the wrong way up, i.e. dividing the percentage change in price by the percentage change in quantity demanded.

C   This answer is arrived at by calculating the percentage change in quantity demanded incorrectly, i.e. (300 – 248) ÷ 248 × 100, which gives a percentage change in quantity demanded of 20.97%.

D   This answer is arrived at by calculating the percentage change in quantity demanded incorrectly as outlined above as well as calculating the percentage change in price incorrectly, i.e. (75p – 82p) ÷ 82p × 100, which gives a percentage change in quantity demanded of –8.54%.

Question 8

A   A rival good means one person's consumption affects the consumption of another individual. Such a good is not a public good. An excludable good means individuals can be prevented from consuming the good if they have not paid for it. Such a good is not a public good.

B   An excludable good cannot be classed as a public good – see above.

C   A rival good cannot be classed as a public good – see above.

D   *Correct answer.* Public goods are both non-excludable (individuals cannot be excluded from the good even if they have not paid for consuming it) and non-rival (the consumption of one individual does not affect the consumption of another).

Question 9

A   This is a positive externalities case. In this circumstance individuals are fully aware of the external benefits but simply ignore them because they do not affect their welfare.

B   *Correct answer.* Because individuals are not fully aware of their own benefits of consuming the good due to information failure they demand a sub-optimal quantity of the good, resulting in under-consumption occurring.

C   As explained above, the market failure is due to information failure here rather than externalities, resulting in under-consumption.

D   Undervaluing private benefits results in under-consumption rather than over-consumption.

Question 10

A   In the positive externalities case the market fails because individuals do not care about the benefits to third parties that derive from the consumption of the good – providing information will not solve the market failure, as individuals already know about their private benefits and no amount of information will make them care about the external benefits.

B   The market fails here because individuals do not care about the harm caused to third parties – providing them with information will be ineffective as it will not stop them from ignoring these external costs, as they are interested only in their own private costs and benefits.

C   In the merit goods case individuals do not realise the full benefits of consuming the good – a positive information campaign detailing the benefits of consumption would be required here.

D   *Correct answer.* The market fails in the demerit goods case because individuals overestimate the benefits of consuming the good. An information campaign detailing the harm of consumption will mean individuals will realise the good is less beneficial to them than they first thought, causing demand to decrease and solving the market failure of over-consumption.

■AS microeconomics Section B

Data response

Airport capacity in the UK

Record numbers of passengers are passing through the UK's major airports. Significant increases in the number of business flights being made to and from fast-growing economies India and China, consumers' growing appetite for short breaks and the increasing cost of domestic rail travel have all placed a strain on the UK's limited airport capacity.

The aviation industry is worth billions of pounds to the UK economy. However, the UK's largest airport, Heathrow, is facing competition from larger airports in Amsterdam (five runways), Paris and Frankfurt (both with four runways) to be considered Europe's leading 'hub' airport.

The government is therefore considering options to expand airport capacity in the UK:

■ *Option 1* – Build a third runway at Heathrow Airport, at a cost of £16 billion. This would create an airport large enough to compete with the major hub airports in the rest of Europe but would require the compulsory purchase of 750 homes in order to create the space needed for the runway.

■ *Option 2* – Build a second runway at Gatwick Airport, at a cost of £9 billion. This is the quickest and cheapest of the options available and would ease capacity concerns but Gatwick would not be a large enough airport to be considered a competitive hub.

■ *Option 3* – Build a new airport in the Thames Estuary at a cost of £45 billion. The most expensive of the options available, this would see a new five-runway airport built in an area in which noise pollution would be at a minimum.

Airlines are hoping the increase in capacity will result in a fall in the landing fees they have to pay to the airports. Landing fees at Heathrow are currently in excess of £20 per passenger, which is putting pressure on the airlines' average costs.

Not everyone is convinced by plans to increase airport capacity. Some argue that the huge cost involved cannot be justified at a time when increased spending on healthcare and education is desperately needed. Others argue that the environmental impact from increasing the number of flights in the UK would mean expansion would cause more harm than good to UK citizens.

(a) 'Increasing capacity at Gatwick is the cheapest of the options available.' Explain whether this is a positive or normative statement. (2 marks)

e A definition and application are required here.

(b) Explain, using a PPF diagram, the opportunity cost involved in undertaking spending on increasing airport capacity in the UK. (4 marks)

e An applied diagram is needed here and should be referred to in your written explanation.

(c) Using the case study, state and explain two factors that have accounted for increased demand for air travel in recent years. (4 marks)

e This question should be answered in two parts – state a determinant and offer an applied explanation before moving on to the second determinant.

(d) Explain what is meant by average costs.

(2 marks)

ⓔ A standard definition is required here, which could be mathematical.

(e) Explain the negative externalities of production that could be generated from expanding airport capacity.

(3 marks)

ⓔ More than one example of negative externalities should be offered here. Remember to apply your answer clearly to the aviation industry.

(f) Evaluate which of the three proposals represents the most desirable policy intervention from the perspective of an economist seeking to maximise social welfare.

(10 marks)

ⓔ The directive word 'evaluate' means a two-sided answer is required here. You will need to use economic theory to support the arguments referred to in the case study.

Student A

(a) This is a positive statement as it is a statement of fact which can be objectively tested. It is possible to get estimates of the cost of all three options and see whether Gatwick represents the cheapest option.

ⓔ 2/2 marks awarded. Student A explains what a positive statement is and then applies how the statement in the question could be objectively tested.

(b)

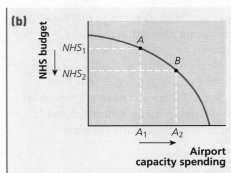

Increasing spending on airport capacity will be at the opportunity cost of spending on the NHS.

ⓔ 3/4 marks awarded. The diagram is correct but there is no reference to it in the written analysis. The analysis should recognise that by spending (A2 – A1) more on airport capacity (NHS1 – NHS2), less can be spent on the NHS – NHS spending has to be sacrificed.

(c) A greater appetite for short breaks has increased demand for air travel, as people are travelling abroad more regularly.

An increase in the cost of domestic rail travel has also boosted demand for air travel. As rail and air travel are substitutes in some instances (e.g. London to Edinburgh journeys), an increase in the price of the substitute will cause demand for air travel to increase.

ℯ 3/4 marks awarded. The second statement includes an applied link to the non-price factor (price of substitutes). This is missing in the first statement – changes in tastes and fashion should be mentioned.

(d) Average cost is equal to Total cost divided by Output.

ℯ 2/2 marks awarded.

(e) Expanding airport capacity will result in increased air traffic, which will generate several harm to third parties. Residents close to the airport will experience greater noise pollution as a result of more planes flying overhead. Moreover, the environment could be damaged by a higher level of emissions, which in the long term could harm all citizens through global warming.

ℯ 3/3 marks awarded. Clear identification of who the third parties are and what harm they will suffer.

(f) Option 3 – building a new Thames Estuary airport – appears to be the option which will best maximise social welfare. This is because building the airport here, away from the congested areas of Heathrow and Gatwick, will generate less external cost – fewer third parties will suffer from the noise pollution generated from air traffic. Moreover, the fact that this airport will have five runways, in comparison with three at Heathrow or two at Gatwick, will enable it to compete effectively as a hub airport with its European competitors, which could generate more employment and growth for the UK economy.

However, given the government's scarce resources, this may not be the best option. The government does not have an unlimited budget and this option is by far the most expensive. It therefore generates a significant opportunity cost, as many other public services will have to be sacrificed in order to fund it.

ℯ 5/10 marks awarded. There is a good two-sided analysis here exploring both the costs and benefits of Option 3, but the evaluation is only reasonable. This is because while the answer reaches a conclusion that Option 3 is the most effective, this is not justified. The student needs to present a reasoned conclusion which considers the relative merits of Option 3 in comparison with an alternative option to justify why Option 3 is the most effective.

Questions & Answers

(a) This is a positive statement as the extract says Gatwick is the cheapest option.

ⓔ **1/2 marks awarded.** Correct identification that it is a positive statement but the explanation is incorrect – the fact that it can be found in the extract isn't alone proof that it is a positive statement.

(b) In order to spend more on increasing airport capacity, funds have to be reallocated from the NHS and other core public services such as education, meaning spending in other areas has to be sacrificed.

ⓔ **2/4 marks awarded.** Good written analysis but lacks a diagram – you must always include a diagram whenever you are asked for one.

(c) The development of China and India has resulted in incomes in these two countries rising, thus increasing demand for air travel from consumers in these countries. A decrease in the price of complements has also increased demand for air travel, as these goods are jointly demanded.

ⓔ **2/4 marks awarded.** While a decrease in the price of complements is a valid non-price factor, there is no reference to it in the extract so it cannot be credited here.

(d) Average cost is the cost of producing one more unit of output.

ⓔ **0/2 marks awarded.** The student has confused average cost and marginal cost here.

(e) There will be more CO_2 emissions as a result of more aeroplanes flying as well as more noise pollution.

ⓔ **1/3 marks awarded.** Identification of the harm of increased air travel but no explanation of why these represent negative externalities.

(f) Option 1 will generate a significant external cost to the 750 households forced to move out in order for the new runway at Heathrow to be built.

Option 2 is the cheapest and so will generate the least opportunity cost, but Gatwick will remain too small to compete as a hub airport.

Option 3 will create the largest airport and will generate the least external cost.

ⓔ **3/10 marks awarded.** These are all correct statements but there is no comparison between options, nor a judgement as to which of these options is the most desirable. This answer demonstrates a reasonable level of knowledge and understanding without offering economic analysis.

AS microeconomics Section C

Essay questions

Question 1

In 2012, the Scottish Parliament passed legislation introducing a minimum price on alcohol, a good which is thought to generate significant negative externalities of consumption.

Evaluate, using an appropriate diagram(s), the effectiveness of minimum pricing as a method of correcting market failure in the market for alcohol.

(20 marks)

(e) The answer must begin with an analysis of how minimum pricing can overcome the market failure associated with negative externalities of consumption (which may be illustrated with an externalities diagram). It must include a relevant minimum price diagram illustrating the impact of the policy. The limitations of the policy must then be considered before reaching a judgement about the effectiveness of the policy, which could include consideration of alternative solutions.

Student A

The consumption of alcohol can often be seen to harm third parties who are outside of the market transaction. When deciding whether to consume alcohol, individuals will be thinking about the private benefits they derive from consumption. They will ignore the harm their consumption might cause to third parties, such as the antisocial behaviour that may result in damage to property and noise disturbance. (a) Because of the harm caused to third parties, the marginal social benefit will be less than the marginal private benefit of consumption. If left to the free market, the equilibrium consumption will occur at the point where MPB = MPC, resulting in a consumption level of Q_1 as illustrated in the diagram below.

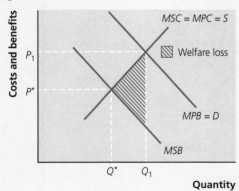

This level of consumption is clearly above the socially optimal level of consumption at Q^* (where MSB = MSC), creating a situation of over-consumption. This means the market fails to achieve allocative efficiency and justifies intervention by the government to try to reduce the size of the welfare loss. b

Introducing a minimum price for alcohol could be seen as an effective solution to overcome the market failure. By preventing firms from selling a unit of alcohol for below a price of P_2, there will be a contraction along the demand curve, as some consumers will reduce their consumption of alcohol due to the higher price. c This will result in a new consumption level at Q_2, as shown in the diagram below. Because the minimum price will have reduced the level of consumption, it could be seen as effective in overcoming the over-consumption problem and therefore reducing the level of allocative inefficiency in the market. d

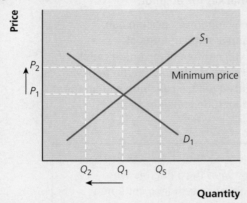

However, the effectiveness of minimum pricing depends upon a number of factors. e If the demand for alcohol is price inelastic, then imposing a minimum price is unlikely to reduce the level of consumption by a significant amount, as illustrated below.

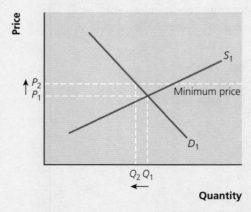

Despite imposing a minimum price at P_2 well above the market equilibrium price of P_1, it results in only a marginal decrease in the level of consumption (from Q_1 to Q_2). Under these circumstances the policy would be ineffective in solving the market failure of over-consumption, as it does not significantly reduce the level of consumption. f

Moreover, minimum pricing will be effective only if it can be properly enforced. There are thousands of licensed sellers of alcohol across the country, meaning it is going to be very difficult for the government to ensure all of them are following the rules. If there are a number of small off-licences selling alcohol at a price below the minimum, this will render the policy ineffective as individuals will still have access to cheap alcohol. g

In judgement, introducing a minimum price for alcohol is unlikely to be an effective solution to the market failure generated by the negative externalities of consumption. While it will help reduce the level of alcohol consumption, this is not well targeted because it is unlikely to reduce the consumption of those individuals actually causing harm to third parties – individuals whose alcohol consumption results in them damaging property are more likely to be addicted to alcohol and, therefore, continue to purchase it even at the higher price the minimum price creates. h Therefore, it may be more effective to increase the severity of the punishments faced by those who display anti-social behaviour as a result of drinking alcohol, as this is a more direct solution, which targets those causing the harm to third parties. i

e **18/20 marks awarded.** a The student offers clear examples of the negative externalities of consumption applied to the market for alcohol. b There is a strong analysis detailing why government intervention can be justified, with an accurate diagram used to explain how the divergence between social and private benefits results in an allocatively inefficient outcome. c By explaining the contraction along the demand curve that results from the minimum price being imposed, the student clearly explains how consumer behaviour is altered by the policy. d An accurate minimum price diagram is used to support strong written analysis to clearly show that the market failure of over-consumption has been corrected by reducing the level of consumption. Reference to the increased supply of alcohol that will result, as illustrated in the diagram, and the potential for black markets this generates would have strengthened the answer.

e The student then clearly demonstrates they are moving on to the other side of the argument by providing a link sentence. f Well-developed evaluation is offered, with a diagram used to support the point that a minimum price will be ineffective when demand is price inelastic. g Offering a second evaluative point deepens the discussion. h The nuanced judgement identifies the fact that even a reduction in consumption will not necessarily solve the specific market failure that occurs here. i Consideration of an alternative policy helps contextualise the limitations of the rejected policy, although recognition that this alternative policy also has its flaws would have propelled the answer to full marks.

Student B

Introducing a minimum price for alcohol will help solve the over-consumption that exists in the market for alcohol. 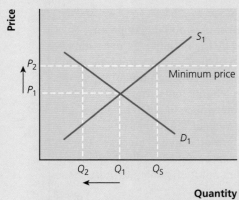 a This can be illustrated in the diagram below, where the marginal private benefit of consumption exceeds the marginal private cost. b

The result is that the level of consumption will be too high at Q_1 because individuals ignore the harm caused to third parties by consuming the good. c

The imposition of a minimum price will make alcohol more expensive. This will cause the consumption of alcohol to fall, as fewer individuals will be willing to purchase alcohol at a higher price. d

However, introducing a minimum price can cause a number of problems. One such problem is that it is difficult to know what level the minimum price should be set at. If it is set at too low a level, then consumption will not fall by enough; if set at too high a level, government failure could result as consumption will be reduced below the social optimum. e Moreover, the higher prices firms can receive from alcohol could result in a situation of excess supply; there is a risk a black market will result as a consequence, where alcohol is available for sale illegally below the minimum price. f

---

ⓔ **9/20 marks awarded.** a The student recognises that the market failure that occurs in this market is one of over-consumption. b The statement that MPB exceeds MPC is incorrect – there is a divergence between social and private benefits, not private benefits and costs. c An accurate negative externalities of consumption diagram is presented and over-consumption is correctly identified, but an application to the alcohol market would improve the answer. For example, the student should give examples of some of the harm alcohol consumption causes to third parties. d While the correct impact of a minimum price is identified and the student does explain how this will result in reduced consumption of alcohol, it is lacking a correct diagram to illustrate this point. The analysis would also be strengthened if the policy outcome was linked back to the initial market failure, explaining how this results in an outcome of improved allocative efficiency. e The evaluative point about it being difficult to know at what level to set the minimum price is well explained. It could be strengthened by explaining that this is because it is hard to estimate the size of the negative externality, along with a diagram to illustrate this. ⓘ The student recognises that a minimum price could result in black markets forming. A diagram illustrating the problems associated with disequilibrium would improve this point. The answer is missing a clear judgement reaching a conclusion as to whether or not minimum pricing represents an effective solution to this problem.

Question 2

Each year thousands of people are hospitalised in Britain because of flu. A number of supermarkets and major chemists offer customers a flu jab for approximately £15.

Evaluate, using an appropriate diagram(s), the effectiveness of an information campaign by the government designed to promote the benefits of the flub jab as a method of correcting market failure resulting from information failure. (20 marks)

e A two-sided discussion is required here, which includes diagrammatic analysis of how information provision may overcome market failure in the merit goods case. Limitations of the policy should be considered and the answer must reach a judgement about its overall effectiveness, which could be compared with alternative solutions.

Student A

Flu jabs could be seen to be merit goods – consuming them brings more benefits to consumers than they realise. This is because many individuals are myopic, meaning they do not fully account for long-term benefits which do not directly enhance their welfare in the short run. For example, an individual may decide that as they are currently feeling in good health there is no need to pay £15 to have a flu jab. When they find themselves suffering from flu three months later they will regret the decision to have not purchased a flu jab. If the individual had not undervalued the benefits of the flu jab they would have purchased it. Because they do not do so the market fails. **a**

The government could introduce an information campaign to advertise the benefits of getting a flu jab. For example, they could arrange for posters to be displayed in doctors' surgeries and on the back of buses outlining the significantly decreased risk of flu which results from having the flu jab. As this will make individuals more aware of the benefits they will derive from having a flu jab, the demand for flu jabs will increase. The demand curve will shift to the right from D_1 to D_2, with the quantity of flu jabs consumed increasing from Q_1 to Q_2 as illustrated in the diagram below.

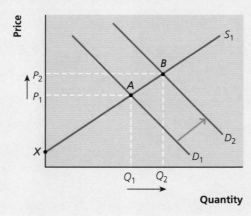

This will solve the market failure in this market as more people will be receiving flu jabs. b However, this depends upon the effectiveness of the advertising campaign. Only a fraction of the population is likely to see these adverts – lots of people rarely visit a doctor and the government is unlikely to be able to afford to advertise on buses around the country, as the opportunity cost of such expenditure would be too great.

Moreover, the advertising is unlikely to change the behaviour of many individuals – there is endless conflicting advice in the public domain about the relative merits of different healthcare treatments, which will leave many individuals confused and unlikely to follow this latest piece of guidance being offered. If this is the case the demand curve is unlikely to shift to the right by much, meaning consumption doesn't increase by much and the policy is not particularly effective in overcoming market failure. c

In conclusion, it is likely information provision will be effective in increasing the consumption of flu jabs and therefore overcoming the market failure which exists. This is because while some individuals may not see or understand the adverts, those who do see them will demand more jabs as a result. However, this depends upon the extent to which the market failure in this instance derives from information failure or positive externalities.

It could be argued that a major benefit of having a flu jab could be that third parties are less likely to catch the flu from the person who has had the jab. An information campaign would be ineffective in increasing consumption in this instance because no amount of information would make individuals care about benefits to third parties. d

---

e 16/20 marks awarded. a The student offers a well-applied example of why individuals undervalue the private benefits of a flu jab. However, they should explain clearly how this links to market failure – offering more technical analysis explaining how the demand curve is below the optimal level leading to under-consumption in the free market would help. b An accurate and well-explained diagram is used to illustrate how information provision will increase the number of flu jabs consumed, but again reference to the fact that this solves the under-consumption problem would be advisable. c The student offers two well-developed criticisms of the information provision solution. d The answer offers strong evaluation with a reasoned judgement, which recognises that information provision is effective only in overcoming a particular type of market failure.

Student B

There is information failure in the market for flu jabs because these jabs generate private and external benefits. When an individual gets a jab their risk of getting the flu is diminished, which is a private benefit to the individual as it improves their health and well-being. However, when an individual gets a jab this benefits society more widely, as third parties who come into contact with the individual are less likely to catch the flu from the immunised individual. Because individuals are not aware of these external benefits, flu jabs will be under-consumed, meaning there is market failure. Some individuals will also not be aware of their private benefits, causing further under-consumption.

A government information campaign which promotes the benefits of flu jabs will increase the demand for flu jabs, as individuals are now more aware of the benefits of consumption. As illustrated in the diagram below, this will cause the demand for flu jabs to increase, resulting in consumption rising and therefore correcting the market failure of under-consumption.

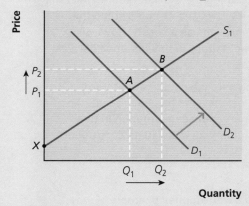

However, the effectiveness of information provision depends upon whether it does actually result in a significant increase in the demand for the product. There are already regular news stories about the flu and individuals who would benefit from having a jab therefore probably already know about it. If this is the case then the policy will be effective only if consumers are not acting rationally – if they are and are already aware of the benefits of consumption then the information provision will not increase the consumption of the jabs.

Overall information provision is a better policy than a subsidy because a subsidy will only lower the price of the good, which will have no impact on correcting the market failure as making the good cheaper will not make individuals believe consumption is more beneficial, whereas information provision directly targets the cause of the market failure.

12/20 marks awarded. The student has correctly identified that there is an under-consumption problem but has confused the cause of this. While there might be positive externalities associated with the consumption of flu jabs, this is not as a result of information failure – in the case of externalities, individuals have the information that consumption will affect third parties but ignore this information when making decisions because they care only about their own welfare. Information failure essays must focus on individuals incorrectly estimating the private benefits of consumption – i.e. the merit or demerit good case. ⓑ The merit goods case is briefly referred to but requires a more detailed explanation.

ⓒ The answer offers good analyses of how information provision will increase the demand for the product and therefore solve the market failure of under-consumption. The analysis cannot be considered strong because it does not recognise the difference between the merit good and the positive externalities problem – information provision would not cause the demand curve to shift to the right in the positive externalities case, which this analysis implies. ⓓ Reference to rationality in evaluation is impressive but would benefit from being developed by explaining that we generally assume in Economics that consumers are acting in a way that maximises their own individual welfare.

ⓔ A judgement is reached which suggests that information provision is more effective than a subsidy, but this could be strengthened with recognition that a subsidy would be particularly ineffective in the case of price inelastic demand, as consumption would not rise significantly in this instance when the price decreased. In this instance the only way to increase consumption would be to stimulate a shift in the demand curve, as information provision effectively does.

■ A-level microeconomics Section A

Data response

Centre Film is a small business operating a chain of six cinemas in the South West of England. It has been established for more than two decades but in recent years has been finding its revenues squeezed by the ever increasing dominance of the three major cinema operators, Vue, Cineworld and Odeon, which between them account for more than two-thirds of cinema screens in the UK. Last year, the managing director made the bold decision to close down two cinemas to change the focus of the company to the booming market of online movie streaming, as she believed this would yield greater profits for Centre Film in the long run.

The online movie streaming industry has been booming since 2012. It is a rare success story of rapid growth at a time when real incomes were falling by approximately 3% a year, with subscriber numbers consistently increasing by 15% per annum. This annual increase is expected to continue over the next few years as rising incomes enable more consumers to enter this market place.

Fierce competition between major providers characterises this industry. Netflix, Amazon Instant Video (formally Love Film) and NOW TV (operated by Sky) dominate the market and already have large numbers of subscribers. In May 2014, Netflix took the decision to increase the price of its subscription from £5.99 a month to £6.99. One estimate suggests that the firm lost 800,000 of its 2.9 million subscribers as a result of this price increase.

Since entering the industry last year, Centre Film has charged £4.99 a month to its subscribers. Despite this being cheaper than many of its competitors, the company has been unable to attract a large number of consumers to the service – there are currently only 5,000 subscribers. Part of the reason for this is that Centre Film struggles to get access to the blockbuster hits as early as some of its rivals; Sky's NOW TV service in particular regularly offers subscribers popular releases two months in advance of Centre Film, using its strong negotiating power with the film distributors to gain an advantage over its competitors. Moreover, consumers have increasingly high expectations over the quality of the images provided by the service – the major providers have invested millions developing their user interface for this purpose.

Strong customer satisfaction evidenced from surveys has suggested to the managing director of Centre Film that the company is on the path to success in this industry. Customers have in particular praised the quality of customer service on offer from Centre Film, noting its ability to provide access to niche titles often not accessible on the mainstream platforms.

(a) **Using an example from the stimulus material above, explain how incentives impact on the behaviour of economic agents when deciding how to allocate resources.**

(2 marks)

ⓔ Identify the key incentive that drives firms' behaviour and apply it to the stimulus material.

(b) **Explain, using relevant elasticity calculations, whether Centre Film would be wise to decrease the price of its on-demand service.**

(4 marks)

ⓔ An elasticity calculation is required which must then be interpreted to explain whether prices should be decreased.

(c) Explain, using a relevant diagram, the impact an increase in the popularity of online movie streaming has had on the market for cinemas.   (4 marks)

ⓔ The supply and demand model should be used to explain the impact on the market equilibrium for cinemas of changes in the popularity of online movie streaming.

(d) Evaluate whether online movie streaming services can be categorised as an inferior good.   (8 marks)

ⓔ The directive word 'evaluate' means a two-sided answer is required here. Elasticity calculations could strengthen your answer and a supported judgement should be reached.

(e) Using evidence from the stimulus material, evaluate the extent to which economies of scale represent a significant barrier to Centre Film being able to compete in the online movie streaming industry.   (12 marks)

ⓔ A two-sided answer is required here with a supported judgement. The material in the stimulus should be used on both sides, explaining why economies of scale might and might not make it difficult for Centre Film to compete in the industry.

> ### Student A
>
> **(a)** Centre Film is motivated by maximising profit. The opportunity to earn a greater profit in the online movie streaming industry is what is incentivising the managing director to reallocate resources by closing down cinemas and entering the online movie streaming industry.

ⓔ **2/2 marks awarded.** There is a clear identification of the incentive that determines firms' behaviour – maximising profit – and an example of this behaviour related to the stimulus material is provided.

> **(b)** Netflix PED = % change in quantity demanded ÷ % change in price
>
> % change in QD = (2.1 million – 2.9 million) ÷ 2.9 million × 100 = –27.6%
>
> % change in P = (£6.99 – £5.99) ÷ £5.99 × 100 = 16.7%
>
> PED = –1.65
>
> It would therefore be a bad idea for Centre Film to increase its prices because demand is price elastic, so it would lead to a more than proportional decrease in quantity demanded and result in revenue falling.

ⓔ **2/4 marks awarded.** Price elasticity of demand has been calculated correctly but the subsequent explanation does not answer the question. The student needs to explain whether or not it is a good idea to decrease the price, whereas this answer explains why the price should not be increased.

(c) The demand curve for cinemas will shift to the left from D_1 to D_2 as shown in the diagram below. This will cause the price of cinema tickets to decrease from P_1 to P_2 and the quantity of tickets sold to decrease from Q_1 to Q_2.

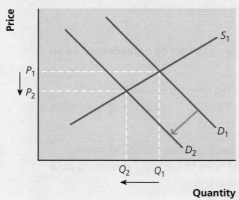

ⓔ **3/4 marks awarded.** An accurate diagram with an accurate explanation of the impact of the change in the equilibrium, but there is no analysis of why changes in the online movie streaming market are causing the demand curve to shift in the cinema market.

(d) Online movie streaming services are inferior goods because they have a negative income elasticity of demand (YED = −5). When incomes were falling by 3% a year, demand was rising by 15%. This suggests that consumers were switching away from going to the cinema to the relatively cheaper option of watching movies online.

However, the extract suggests that demand is set to increase even when incomes are rising in the coming years, which brings this relationship into question. It suggests that ceteris paribus doesn't hold – the initial analysis was based on income being the only variable affecting demand for online movie streaming services, whereas in reality demand was probably increasing at this time not because incomes were falling but because consumer preferences were changing towards watching movies online. The demand for such services could perhaps have risen even quicker if a decrease in income was not partially offsetting the increase in demand coming as a result of the increasing popularity.

In conclusion it is very clear that online movie streaming is not an inferior good. The technology required to take full advantage of a online movie subscription service – a good quality internet connection, an internet-enabled television and a surround-sound system – are all very expensive purchases, meaning as incomes rise and individuals can afford to purchase more of this technology demand for subscriptions is likely to rise.

ⓔ 8/8 marks awarded. An excellent answer which uses the stimulus material to good effect to support the analysis on both sides. YED is calculated correctly and the weakness of such estimates is recognised. The answer reaches a clear and well-supported judgement.

(e) As stated in the extract, Centre Film is struggling to compete with the major providers because it is not able to get hold of the new releases early enough. This is an example of purchasing economies of scale. Large firms such as NOW TV are more important customers to film distributors and so are able to negotiate better terms than Centre Film, such as earlier access to the blockbuster films and potentially purchasing the rights to showing the films at a cheaper price. This means NOW TV have lower long run average costs as a result of their large scale of output so can charge lower prices than Centre Film, making it difficult for Centre Film to compete.

However, given this is an online industry, it could be argued that there are not as significant economies of scale as in the cinema industry, where Centre Film would have to pay significantly higher prices for expensive technology such as cinema screens than Cineworld because it is operating on a smaller scale. Moreover, the large providers such as Netflix may experience diseconomies of scale, where their average costs might actually rise as a result of their high level of output. This may be because workers are demotivated because they do not feel like an important part of the business, meaning they give poor quality service to customers.

In conclusion, I believe economies of scale are going to make it difficult for Centre Film to compete in this market. Ultimately consumers will choose a service based on the films they can watch and, given many film distributors often make exclusive deals for shows with the major providers, it is going to be difficult for Centre Film to compete as they simply do not have the same bargaining power.

ⓔ 11/12 marks awarded. Purchasing economies of scale are well applied to the industry and there is strong analysis of why the lack of such economies of scale will make it difficult for Centre Film to compete. Recognising diseconomies of scale exist is important, but this could be developed by explaining how this may mean the small scale of Centre Film isn't necessarily a disadvantage, as there may be some advantages to operating on a small scale. The evaluation is strong as there is a supported judgement which recognises how significant economies of scale are in this industry.

Student B

(a) Individuals and firms are motivated by their own self-interest. Individuals are incentivised to behave in a way which maximises their own satisfaction and firms are incentivised to allocate resources to the production of the good or service which results in them getting the most profit.

ⓔ **1/2 marks awarded.** Good explanation of the impact of incentives on the behaviour of economic agents but this is not applied to the stimulus material.

(b) PED = −1.65.

Yes, Centre Film should decrease the price as Revenue = Price × Quantity, so more revenue can be made by decreasing the price.

ⓔ **3/4 marks awarded.** The answer is correct but the chain of analysis is missing – the PED figure needs to be interpreted as being elastic, with an explanation that this means a small decrease in price will cause a large increase in quantity demanded and will therefore increase revenue. You should also always include your working to show how you calculated the PED – if you make a mistake with your final answer you can still get marks if you have followed the right methodology.

(c) Online movie viewing and going to the cinema are substitutes. As watching movies online is becoming more popular it is becoming less desirable to go to the cinema. These changes in tastes and fashion are causing the demand curve for cinema going to shift to the left from D_1 to D_2.

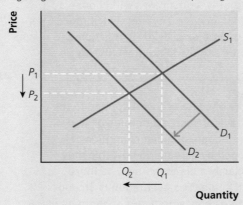

ⓔ **2/4 marks awarded.** Good explanation of why the demand curve shifts, but there is no explanation of the actual impact on the market – what happens to price and quantity must be considered when answering this question.

(d) When an individual experiences a decrease in their level of income they are unlikely to be able to afford to go to the cinema, so will switch to the relatively cheaper substitute of watching movies online. This means online movie subscription services are likely to be inferior goods, as demand rises when income falls and will fall when income rises, as individuals will then switch back to going to the cinema when they can afford it. I have calculated from the information in the case study that the YED is –5, which suggests it is an inferior good.

However, the fact that demand is expected to rise when income rises in the future suggests that the income elasticity of demand may be changing from negative to positive and that, while the good may have been an inferior good in the past, it is now changing to be a normal or luxury good.

🄴 **3/8 marks awarded.** The initial analysis interpreting the negative YED estimate is correct, but the discussion is confused. The student does not recognise that the fact that demand will carry on rising when income rises is more likely to suggest there is another factor causing demand to rise rather than the relationship between income and quantity demanded actually changing.

(e) The large firms in this industry benefit from technological economies of scale. Because of their large scale of output they are able to spread the cost of expensive technological developments (such as improving the quality of images for subscribers) over a large number of units of output. This is something Centre Film is unable to do because it simply lacks the scale to do so, meaning its customers do not have access to the high-quality service offered by its competitors. Financial economies of scale are also important here. The large firms such as Amazon Instant Video will be able to borrow to fund these technological developments at lower interest rates than Centre Film because there is less risk to the bank of them not paying the money back. This means large firms have a lower long run average cost than Centre Film.

However, one could argue operating on a smaller scale actually benefits Centre Film. As mentioned in the case study, they are able to respond quickly to consumer needs and do things such as provide access to niche films – it is impossible for the large companies to offer this level of customer service when they have millions of subscribers.

Overall economies of scale are not a major barrier to Centre Film being able to compete – there are many online-based firms which started out small which were able to grow to become big over time.

🄴 **9/12 marks awarded.** There is strong analysis of two economies of scale but the student would benefit from explaining how these higher average costs experienced by Centre Film make it difficult for the company to compete. There is a strong explanation of why the small scale of output may benefit Centre Film; a technical link to diseconomies of scale would improve this analysis. A clear judgement is reached, but it could be better supported – a generic statement that many tech-based firms start small is not proof that Centre Film will be able to successfully compete with incumbent firms.

■ A-level microeconomics Section B

Quantitative essay question

When the National Health Service (NHS) was launched in 1948, it had an annual budget of approximately £9 billion at today's prices. The NHS budget now exceeds £115 billion, with the mainstream political parties all agreeing even further increases in the budget are needed to provide a good quality service.

Evaluate, using an appropriate diagram(s), whether healthcare should be privatised.

(25 marks)

ⓔ A two-sided discussion is required here which considers the arguments both for and against healthcare being privatised. Diagrams should be used to support your analysis before you make a supported judgement that reaches a conclusion about which model of healthcare provision is the most desirable.

Student A

Healthcare should be privatised because government provision is simply too expensive and wasteful. When a good or service is provided for free (as it is currently), consumers who derive virtually no benefit from consuming healthcare services will consume the service because they are not charged anything for doing so. This is illustrated on the diagram below, where consumption takes place at the bottom of the demand curve at Q_1.

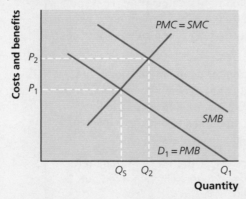

This creates a situation of significant over-consumption – consumption is well above the social optimum of Q^*. ⓐ Evidence of this in the NHS can be seen at present, where people call for ambulances or visit A&E when their condition is not serious enough to warrant hospital treatment. ⓑ This is an inefficient use of scarce resources as too many resources are being allocated towards the provision of healthcare. When healthcare is privatised, this wastage will be eliminated as when people have to pay for a service they are less likely to abuse it and will only consume healthcare when the benefit they derive from doing so is at least equal to the cost, meaning consumption will reduce to Q_M. ⓒ Moreover, the profit incentive private firms have is likely to improve the efficiency of

---

provision, helping to reduce the cost of healthcare provision and in doing so improving productive and allocative efficiency in the market. d

However, there are a number of problems with privatisation. When healthcare is charged at a price of P_M, there will clearly be some individuals who are priced out of the market, unable to afford the cost of the service. Many would argue healthcare is a basic right in a developed country and that it is not acceptable for some individuals to potentially die because they are denied access to healthcare they cannot afford. Ensuring access to all citizens is therefore an important argument in favour of state provision and against privatisation. e

While there are ways around this problem in a private system by, for example, offering the poorest in society free access to private healthcare, fragmenting the system in this way can be extremely expensive and end up costing the government significantly more per capita than it would have done to provide it free for the whole population – a good example of this is the healthcare system in America, which is not run by the government and yet still incurs a huge cost to taxpayers. f

To conclude, healthcare is ultimately too important a service to privatise. While there might be some inefficiency involved in state provision, this is preferable to some individuals missing out on healthcare entirely because they cannot afford it, as would be the case in a fully privatised system. It may be that introducing elements of charging in the NHS may be the best solution to reduce the ever increasing cost of the service – for example, charging patients for missed doctors' appointments may go some way to making individuals value the service closer to the cost of providing it. g

e 22/25 marks awarded. a There is strong technical analysis explaining how state provision of healthcare results in significant over-consumption, with good use of a diagram to support this. b This is well applied to healthcare and makes a strong argument for privatisation. c The analysis that privatisation will reduce consumption is solid, but the answer could be improved by some reference back to this consumption point at a later stage, recognising that this consumption point is below the socially optimum level. d A further strong argument in favour of privatisation is made in terms of the improved efficiency it brings.

e The arguments against privatisation are well made, with reference to the important equity vs. efficiency debate. f The explanation of the problems with a fragmented healthcare system using the example of America provides an excellent context to the answer. g A strong judgement is reached, which recognises that a solution that involves elements of market and state provision may be the most desirable. The arguments made throughout this essay are very strong, but it is unwise to have no mention of the merit good or positive externality elements of healthcare, as these are core underlying principles to this debate. The diagram implies knowledge of this, but there should be more explicit consideration within the essay.

Student B

One of the main advantages of privatising healthcare is the benefits increased competition will bring to consumers. When the NHS is replaced with a number of private healthcare providers, these providers will be competing with each other for customers. This is likely to result in an improved quality service for consumers – hospitals are likely to offer reduced waiting times for operations, better quality hospital food, etc. in order to attract patients to their hospital. Moreover, consumers will now be able to choose between multiple providers – increased choice will improve consumer welfare as they will be able to choose the provider which suits them best. For example, in a privatised system there may be more doctors' surgeries open at weekends and evenings, which will benefit those patients who work full time. a

However, healthcare is a merit good with positive externalities which will therefore be under-consumed if privatised. Because of information failure, individuals are not fully aware of the benefits they will derive from consuming healthcare; if they realised these benefits they would demand more healthcare. Moreover, individuals ignore the benefits to third parties that are derived from their consumption of healthcare; examples include improved GDP which comes from having a healthier and more productive workforce and less risk of others getting ill as a result of the individual consuming healthcare. Both of these factors mean healthcare will be under-consumed if privatised at Q_M in the diagram below, which is below the socially optimal level of consumption at Q^*. This is an argument against privatising healthcare to ensure there is not any under-consumption. b

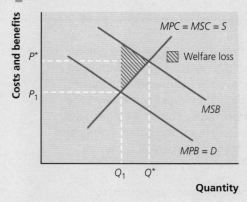

e **15/25 marks awarded.** a There is a good analysis of the benefits to consumers that will result from privatisation. However, this would be strengthened if the key issue raised in the question – the ever increasing cost of healthcare provision – was considered. b There is a reasonable discussion of the drawbacks of privatisation, with good use of the diagram to explain the merit good and positive externalities nature of healthcare. However, the answer lacks a judgement explaining what the student believes to be the best method of providing healthcare.

■ A-level microeconomics Section C

Essay question

Between 1978 and 1995, China's output was growing at an average of 8% per year at a time when it was transitioning from a command to a market-based economy. It is today the world's second largest economy.

Evaluate the extent to which market economies are the most effective way to allocate resources.

(25 marks)

Student A

A market economy can be defined as an economic system where resources are owned and allocated by private individuals and firms. One of the main advantages of this system is the efficiency it creates. Private individuals and firms are driven by their own self-interest. We assume for firms that this usually represents profit. This is therefore likely to result in a more efficient use of resources because firms will look to reduce any wastage, knowing that doing so will increase their level of profit. This is different from command economies, where it is likely some factors of production will be employed inefficiently because there is no profit incentive to eliminate these inefficiencies. a

Moreover, the price mechanism in the market economy ensures allocative efficiency is achieved. Command economies are characterised by surpluses or shortages of products because production decisions are taken at central boards. In a market economy, a shortage would quickly be eliminated. This is because in a situation of excess demand, producers would raise their prices, which would incentivise more producers to enter the market, causing an extension along the supply curve until market equilibrium was reached. This would ensure more scarce resources were allocated to the production of the good or service and enable allocative efficiency to be achieved. There is no adjustment mechanism present in a command economy, meaning disequilibrium is likely to result in the long term. b

However, there are several instances in which the market economy will not allocate resources efficiently. For example, in the case of public goods, the free-rider problem means no individuals will have an incentive to pay for the product knowing they cannot be excluded from its consumption if they have not paid, enabling them to 'free ride' on someone else's consumption. The result of this is that public goods will not be provided in the free market at all, even though they give benefit to consumers. c Moreover, in the case of information failure or externalities, the market mechanism will not achieve an allocatively efficient outcome because the socially optimum level of output does not occur at the point where marginal private benefits are equal to marginal private costs. In the case of education, for example, there would be under-provision in the free market because individuals will not take into account the wider benefits to the economy which result from them being more educated (in terms of the higher tax revenues the government will receive in the future from the individual being in high-paid employment). Thus, just as in a command economy, the market economy can also be vulnerable to a misallocation of resources. d

In conclusion, it is fair to say that market economies are generally the most effective method of allocating resources in an economy. This is because incentives are crucial to the behaviour of economic agents; the market economy provides a powerful profit incentive which ensures the economy's scarce resources are not wasted. However, given there are some instances in which the market economy fails, it is clear that a mixed economy – where resources are owned and allocated by a combination of private firms and individuals and the government – delivers the best of both worlds. e

e **24/25 marks awarded.** a There is strong analysis of how the profit incentive results in a more efficient use of scarce resources in a market economy. b A technical analysis of this is then offered by explaining how the price mechanism serves to deliver an allocatively efficient outcome. A diagram showing the adjustment to equilibrium would have made this analysis even stronger. c There is a strong discussion of the limitations of the market mechanism, with a powerful explanation of how public goods will not be provided at all in a market economy. d Considering the flaws of the market in allocating goods where information failure or externalities exist provides a further argument for some form of government intervention. e The judgement is very strong, reaching a well-considered conclusion that the market economy is a preferable way of allocating most resources but that some element of government intervention is desirable.

Student B

Consumer choice is a major advantage of the market economy. In command economies all resources are owned and allocated by the government, meaning there is little variety for consumers. In a market economy there are often several different firms producing the same product; this enhances consumer welfare as they are able to choose the goods and services which best meet their needs or wants. a In market economies production also tends to take place more efficiently and at a lower cost, which is crucial if countries want to be internationally competitive in the export market. b

However, a major criticism of the market economy is that it can create inequality. Whereas in a command economy the owners of resources are concerned with the welfare of the whole population when making decisions as to how to allocate resources, in a market economy the owners of resources make decisions based on maximising their own welfare. This can result in an outcome in which resources are too heavily concentrated in the hands of a wealthy elite in society, with poverty resulting for those who do not have access to key resources. c There are also short-term problems which are likely to be generated in the transition from a command economy to a market economy, with many workers likely to face unemployment as firms look to improve efficiency. d

Overall the market economy is the most efficient way of allocating resources because of the improved efficiency it brings. This can be evidenced by the fact that the biggest economies in the world can be seen to be heavily reliant on markets for their success. e

ⓔ 18/25 marks awarded. a There is a strong analysis detailing the improved choice that consumers enjoy in a market economy. b The point that a market economic system is likely to be important in being internationally competitive is valid, but the explanation as to why production would be more efficient than in a command economy is lacking; the profit incentive should be mentioned. c There is a very good discussion about how inequality is likely to result in a market economy, suggesting that a command economy has the potential to achieve a fairer outcome for society. d Reference to the short-term transitional problems is well made and could be strengthened if the problems the former Soviet Union countries faced in transitioning were mentioned. e The answer reaches a judgement which explains why the student believes a market economy is the most efficient way of allocating resources, but this would benefit from being more technical – simply recognising that most of the world's biggest economies use markets is not in itself proof that this is the most efficient way of allocating resources.

Knowledge check answers

1 Labour – wage, capital – interest, land – rent, enterprise – profit.
2 There is no opportunity cost to increasing the output of either good as there are spare factors of production, meaning to increase the output of one good, factors of production do not have to be reallocated away from the other good.
3 Countries can become vulnerable to changes in consumer demand – if they specialise in the production of a product that loses popularity then GDP could be significantly harmed. Countries can also become over-reliant on other nations for the supply of essential goods and services.
4 Households will be incentivised to consume more of the good as the opportunity cost of its consumption will have fallen. Firms will be incentivised to produce less of the good – there is now less return to be made from allocating scarce resources to this product.
5 Privatisation is likely to improve efficiency – firms now have a profit incentive and so are likely to use their scarce resources more efficiently than before. However, it is likely to result in many workers losing their jobs as firms cut costs in order to maximise profit.
6 Firms may be considering a wide range of objectives, such as developing their brand and building their customer base. These objectives will impact on their decision making and mean they do not necessarily act in a way that is purely profit maximising.
7

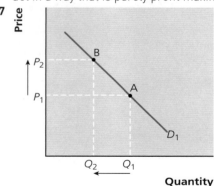

8 The supply curve would shift to the left. Plastic is used to produce mobile phones, meaning the cost of producing the phones would increase. Firms would find it less profitable to supply mobile phones, thus causing supply to decrease.
9 No, because producers simply won't supply the product at a market price lower than the price at which they are willing to supply the product.
10 The government would impose minimum prices on goods for which it wants to reduce consumption. This is most likely to be the case of demerit goods.
11 Easter eggs are a highly seasonal purchase. Demand is not constant throughout the year – it will be very high in the direct build-up to Easter and then will fall dramatically as soon as Easter has passed. This explains why the price of Easter eggs falls so significantly on Easter Monday, as there is a sudden drop in demand on this day.
12 Demand is price inelastic as PED is less than one. This is what you would expect, as while it isn't a necessity good, it takes up a relatively small proportion of disposable income, meaning consumers absorb relatively large percentage increases in price without being priced out of the market.
13 It may still be sensible to decrease the price if there is a non-price factor causing the demand curve to shift to the left or the supply curve to shift to the right. If, for example, the costs of production were to decrease, this would increase supply and result in firms increasing their revenue by lowering the price.
14 % change in QD = (159,000 – 145,000) ÷ 145,000 × 100 = 9.66%
   YED = 9.66% ÷ 4% = **2.42**
15 % change in price of laptops = (£400 – £450) ÷ 450 × 100 = –11.11%
   XED = –7% ÷ –11.11% = **0.63**

   Demand is cross inelastic and these goods are substitutes.
16 % change in QS = (108,000 – 105,000) ÷ 105,000 × 100 = 2.86%
   % change in price = (£225,000 – 205,000) ÷ 205,000 × 100 = 9.76%
   PES = 2.86% ÷ 9.76% = **0.29**
17 Renting the factory is a fixed cost and the ink is a variable cost.
   Average cost = £40,000 ÷ 100,000 = **40p**
18 Purchasing – supermarkets buy large quantities of produce so can, for example, negotiate cheap deals on potatoes with farmers. Managerial – a supermarket employs a big enough staff to have specialist workers, such as a specialist fruit and vegetables team. Technical – supermarkets find it cost efficient and have the funds to invest in technology such as self-service checkouts.
19 Suppose the manager of one of a large supermarket's chain of stores was approached by

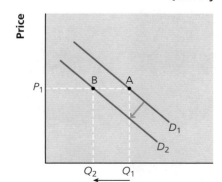

a local farmer offering very cheap rates on fruit and vegetables. Because of the complex contracts a large supermarket is likely to have in place, the manager is unlikely to have the authority to make the decision and will have to consult their manager, who will have to consult their manager. By the time the decision is made the local farmer may well have sold his produce to a rival, smaller, firm.

20 A growth in the size of the industry will mean more people know about the good or service, which may generate demand for the individual firm without it having to invest in costly advertising.

21 Social welfare would improve if consumption increased – too few scarce resources are being allocated to the product.

22 Third parties have the potential to be harmed when other individuals consume alcohol – this could be in the form of antisocial behaviour which results in damage to property or noise pollution. These external costs will not be taken into account in the market transaction.

23 The owner of the car will know much more about the reliability of the car than the potential buyer does. The problem here is that the owner with an unreliable car is unlikely to tell the buyer about this. The result is that buyers are taking a risk when buying a second-hand car, which is why they are willing to pay so much less for one than for a new car.

24 When demand is price inelastic, the equilibrium quantity does not fall much in response to a change in price. This means a very large tax would need to be imposed to overcome the over-consumption or over-production problem.

25 The government would buy up stock. This would increase the demand for the agricultural product, shifting the demand curve to the right and increasing the price.

Index

Note: **Bold** page numbers indicate defined terms.

Index